SHAMELESS/LIMITLESS

SELECTED POSTERS & TEXTS
2008–2020

Kevin, this has turned into quite the sizeable project. And so, right off the top, let's talk stats. How many events are represented here? How many contributors are included? How many designers are featured? What about guest texts?

Norman, it definitely has. The project started with rather vague parameters, and the sheer scope of the undertaking took quite some time to reveal itself. As it stands, it looks like 219 event posters will be featured, made by 130 different designers, for events spread over 41 venues which included contributions — be they performances, DJ sets, stand-up comedy or whatever else may have seemed like a good idea at the time — from around 400 projects. Further to that, there are over 100 event texts, and 24 guest contributions.

It's worth mentioning that this isn't the exhaustive catalogue of Shameless/Limitless events over the years — that tally would total closer to 550. Rather, this is a collection of selected designs and events which nicely encapsulates the S/L experience.

That is indeed a lot to dig out and put together. Somebody's into archival perfection, huh? Is it passion or discipline or OCD?

While I didn't envision my archiving ability to be a talking point surrounding this monster project, kind words are always appreciated so I'll take 'em where I can get 'em. As for archiving as a passion or OCD playing a role: I like my desktop as tidy as the next person, and it takes a certain amount of organizational prowess to keep an operation like this up and running.

When putting on shows, do you mostly focus on the specific night or do you have a legacy in mind? A Shameless/Limitless *Gesamtkunstwerk*, a long tail of music-making and community-building?

At the outset, legacy-building was nowhere on my radar. The goal was simply to make things happen. It eventually evolved into making things happen simply, but I'm getting ahead of myself.

I had zero experience in organizing events prior to my June 2008 arrival in Berlin, though it wasn't for lack of enthusiasm. That the city's conditions enabled me to take a shot at promoting shows was sufficiently exciting to focus primarily on the here and now (or there and then, as it were) without considering what would come next.

Things gradually took on more shape, though for a long stretch of time the M.O. remained the in-the-moment celebration or experience of the night itself.

I recall the shock of a seasoned nightlife connoisseur when, in 2015 or '16 — a time that S/L was running upwards of 80 events a year — I told him that I had very little photo documentation of my nights; that the idea was to focus on the experience of the event as it happened, rather than complicating things ("tainting the purity and inhibiting the wild abandon of the party" might be the way it was thought of back then) with cameras.

Which is a very Berlin idea. Somewhat inherent to the notion of partying Shamelessly and Limitlessly. No photos, no regrets.

Well, he told me I'd rue that line of thinking. He might be right. But, as you'll see here, posters and recollections of those times remain.

What about community?

A consideration of community-building and legacy began to factor in more recently, as the scene has grown. Over the course of a couple of years the imagined potential which I saw in the city when I was one of what seemed like only a small handful of players was in some form realized, as new promoters, projects, artists and venues popped up, albeit without the broad cultural embrace I had felt was possible — or even inevitable. As these changes have come to pass it's been a goal to support the work of people who have an interest in contributing to the scene, while also hoping to maintain the continued relevance of S/L within the ever-evolving landscape.

Given that the people who contributed guest texts to the book range from early collaborators to recent Berlin arrivals, from door staff to headliners, it seems like that sense of community is strong.

For sure. It's heart-warming. I think that a lot of the enduring and enthusiastic support is based on understanding the culture of S/L. It's an entity which, among other things, runs on an ample supply of good faith and participant buy-in. The payoff — and this goes for everyone from the performing artist to venue staff to attendees and beyond — is being part of a nightlife experience which isn't governed by the sorts of factors that can often make nights out feel like a consumer experience or a social obligation.

All that being so, some of the texts, especially the ones from Alex Cameron and Max Kaario, really landed nicely with me, as they illustrate an understanding of and appreciation for what's happening on many levels.

Speaking of understanding what's happening, your event invites, some of which are featured in the book, are consistent with the S/L approach of doing things a little differently. Can you explain a how you approach writing them?

To some extent I consider the event text to be an intangible factor in relation to event attendance, much like the day of the week the show is on and the weather when it happens.

I think it would be appropriate to say that I've both overthought and underthought my approach to writing event texts. On the one hand, the irreverent and off the cuff-style writing is intentionally in contrast to both cut and paste "insert bio here" and overwrought artist statement-style invites which tend to be the norm in nightlife. There is, I hope, a refreshing lack of self-seriousness in the tone of the writing; an awareness that the ultimate goal is for people to come together in the service of a good time. The texts don't contain in-jokes, so much as they communicate that the reader is welcome to be in on the joke, should they so desire.

On the other hand, it's been pointed out that for some, especially non-native English speakers, it can often be difficult to figure out just what the hell it is that I'm even talking about. Having re-read so many invites while working on this book, I can see that side of things too.

What this all adds up to insofar as getting people out to the events themselves is anyone's guess.

Beyond the event texts, posters obviously play a significant role in your communication. Is a Shameless/Limitless show only valid with a poster? How come so much of the communication and promotion happens online, yet there's always a printed poster?

I've always considered a poster to be a central part of an event, and so have very much enjoyed incorporating unique, show-specific designs whenever possible. Many of the S/L posters that aren't included in this collection are ones for which agents or management requested that generic press materials be central to the design.

Actually, posters only get printed for shows where the circumstances — generally informed by economics and anticipated attendance — allow for it. Digital-only posters are put to use in online communication across whatever channels are possible.

I have a hard time respecting digital flyers as posters as I think the quality of a physical poster is that one stumbles upon it in an unexpected situation: like on the street, next to others that are advertising porn fairs and yoga schools.

Is that to say that an S/L poster has never appeared betwixt porn fair and yoga school ads in your feed? Bugger — sounds like the algorithm needs yet more of my attention.

Have you physically put up all the real-world posters yourself?

Indeed, I have been responsible for pasting, taping and tacking 99% of the S/L posters which have found a place in Berlin's streets, bar bathrooms and venues. It has been in equal measure a slog and a pleasure, though it's possible that the positive recollections of all those kilometres walked in the rain and cold undercover of the night are brought on by memories of a world that was …

Same goes for sending out event invites? Social media? Hosting the events?

You got it.

It isn't by any grand design that S/L exists as a one-person operation. By nature of the interests I held and the kinds of events I wanted to make happen, things evolved from being part of a very loose party collective to running S/L as a solo operation. It's now been the reality for so long that I've come to embrace it.

So, I have experienced working with you as a designer. Most striking to me is the meticulous briefing you deliver, yet how you then leave total freedom for the design. What's your thought behind this?

I fondly recall your celebration of the briefing for the 9 Years Shameless/Limitless party – which itself became the poster.

The meticulousness of the briefing is informed by experience – remember that this conversation has been initiated hundreds of times. Changes, a couple of which include a frequently chuckle-inducing "No horses, please!" line, or an ask that designers familiarize themselves with the artists who are playing as well as previous S/L posters, have been incorporated as needed.

Beyond that, many factors inform the communication surrounding design, chief among them a hope that the designer views the experience as a pleasurable one which is creatively and socially satisfying.

It's not lost on me that the compensation I offer for design work – particularly in a city as changed as Berlin over the last decade – is unlikely to yield a flurry of interest in working with me. Instead, I'd like to think that general freedom of creative expression (hopefully in the service of a night which the designer would themselves be interested in supporting), alongside a feeling of contributing to an active and welcoming community, is incentive aplenty to get involved.

Do you ever interfere in the design?

Sure, and perhaps not as often as I should have – readers can draw their own conclusions as they page through the book. If I didn't, it was likely a result in keeping with the spirit I just outlined. And if I did, well, here's hoping we're all the better for the outcome it led to.

I think part of the fun of this collection is that not all of the poster artists would define themselves as designers, right? Many of the works seem imperfect or spontaneous, yet passionate. In many of them I feel the excitement of having been asked to make a poster.

In many cases, contributors – and this ranges from designers to DJs to door staff – were approached on the basis of a stated desire to "get involved", friendship, an appreciation for their creative work in general, or a hunch that they might turn in something cool. Oftentimes this has resulted in successful outcomes, and on rare occasions it has even set people off on a new life trajectory. Other times the results have been, shall we say, mixed.

However, it's my feeling that results of a less than superlative nature highlight the beauty of the S/L structure in which the work is being done, as the stakes are generally modest and the audience is, hopefully, supportive. After all, it's the doing that matters most.

Have you ever designed a poster yourself?

I have. In fact, I've designed a lot – the vast majority of which didn't make it into the book. See the confusing case of Shameless/Limitless's shame & limits.

OK, to end I'm gonna ask "that question": What's your all-time favourite poster? Favourite event?

It shouldn't come as news that answering this question is a challenge, partly on account of my diplomatic nature, and also because of the number of factors that go into making a call like that. In an attempt to save this from being a complete non-answer, I will say I'm very happy that some of my favourite and most frequently tapped designers and artists from over the years have contributed words to this book.

Cliché though it may be, they're all meaningful and beautiful in their own way. Most importantly, each one conjures a memory of a time and place when I, alongside a great group of likeminded doers, got to live a life that I had long dreamt of, and which I can now only dream of.

CAFE WARSCHAU

Shameless/Limitless (DJ)

mittwochs @ Cafe Warschau

SHAMELESS
LIMITLESS

Scandanavian Pop. Ye-Ye. SMSH RMXS
and all the rest.

Sonnenallee 27 | U 7/8 Hermannplatz
www.myspace.com/shamesslimitless

CAFE WARSCHAU

Shameless/Limitless (DJ)

Shameless. Limitless.

BLOG HAUS
SOUTHERN SOUL
URBAN VIBES
+ MORE

CAFE WARSCHAU
SONNENNALLE 27
U7/8 HERMANNPLATZ

MITTWOCH ABENDS

EVERETT DARLING
Skiing

Shameless/Limitless is to party as cream is to peach. While you don't need cream to enjoy a peach, it makes the peach so much sweeter. But still not quite as sweet as Kevin — an all-around sweetheart and overall peach.

CAFE WARSCHAU

Shameless/Limitless (DJ)

Shameless limitless.

_Post Punk.
_Authentic Disco.
_Acid Jazz.
_____and all the rest.

Mittwoch Abends.................................
.....Günstig 0,5l Polnisches Bier.....

Cafe Warschau.
Sonnennalle 27.
U-Hermannplatz.

Shameless/Limitless (DJ)

CANCON, SOUL, NEW WAVE AND ALL THE REST

SHAMELESS / LIMITLESS

MITTWOCH ABENDS   CAFÉ WARSCHAU
GÜNSTIG   SONNENNALLE 27
0,5L POLNISCHES BEER   U7/8 HERMANNPLATZ

2009 02 12   YUMA

Shameless/Limitless (DJ)

Kevin Halpin

S
H
L I A
M M
r y M L I E
e U I T E L
q u m T L L E
f 6 t d E S
e 3 e r q E S
q b r s S S
fin l2 tr S S

2009 02 21   L.U.X

       Shameless/Limitless (DJ)
       Nemoi (DJ)
       Professional Youth (DJ)
       VJ Linards

Omer Schwartz

SHAMELESS LIMITLESS
PROFESSIONAL YOUTH
NEMOI
VJ LINARDS

SATURDAY, FEBRUARY 21
L.U.X
SCHLESISCHE STR. 41
U SCHELESISCHE TOR

4

WESTGERMANY

Basketball
Jailhouse Fuck
Shameless/Limitless (DJ)

BASKETBALL (CAN)
JAILHOUSE
FUCK (SWE)

JUNE 30 WESTGERMANY
SKALITZERSTR 133 U1/8 KOTTBUSSER TOR 21:00

2010 07 30   O TANNENBAUM

Mari Me (DJ)
Shameless/Limitless (DJ)
Oh! Mehr! (DJ)

GLORY NIGHTS NEUKÖLLN

**MARI ME
SHAMELESS/LIMITLESS
OH! MEHR!**

FRIDAY 30.07.10 / 22:00
O-TANNENBAUM / SONNENALLEE 27 NEUKÖLLN

WESTGERMANY

Rangleklods
Skiing
Mari Me (DJ)
Bokonon (DJ)
VJ Linards

SHAMELESS
LIMITLESS

RANGLEKLODS (LIVE)
DJ MARI ME
DJ BOKONON
VJ LINARDS
SKIING (LIVE)

FRIDAY JANUARY 14
WEST GERMANY
SKALITZER STR. 133

Mari Me (DJ)
Oh! Mehr! (DJ)
Town's Syndrome (DJ)
Shameless/Limitless (DJ)

SHAME LIMIT
LESS LESS

Sat. Feb. 12

dj MARI ME
OH! MEHR!
dj Town's syndrome
dj shameless
LImItLess

HAUS 1
WATERLOO Ufer
HaLLeSCHeS
TOR
FREE entry

Rangleklods
Basketball
Skiing
Oh! Mehr! (DJ)
Mari Me (DJ)
Bokonon (DJ)

MAY 1. SHAMELESS LIMITLESS

presents:

rAngleKlods

+ basketball~~
~~ + SkiinG~

+ DJs OH! MEHR!
MARI me
BokoNoN

Chez JaCkle
An Der ScHilling Brücke
Terrace Open 18oo-free
CluB Open frOm 22oo -€5/€6

GRAEME MITCHELL
Designer
Shameless/Limitless Co-founder

Shameless/Limitless began post-Artists
Anonymous in Neukölln, in the final
days of summer '08. Gloriously hazy
days, with gloriously hazy ideas —
optimistic times with hopes and dreams
fully intact.

That Cafe Warschau on Sonnenallee had
posted a sign which read "Momentan
suchen wir DJs mit Eigeninitiative,
die Partys organisieren und Musik
auflegen. Falls jemand gute Ideen hat,
bitte ich um einen Anruf" seemed too
good to be true.

Of course, in the end, it was: we were
unceremoniously kicked out after four
nights of parties which more than made
up in enthusiasm what they lacked in
polish. But: the wheels of Shameless/
Limitless were in motion, and it would
take more than one disgruntled venue
operator to stop them …

2011 05 01   CHEZ JACKI

                    Rangleklods
                    Basketball
                    Skiing
                    Oh! Mehr! (DJ)
                    Mari Me (DJ)
                    Bokonon (DJ)

Ryan Hays

SHAMELESS
LIMITLESS

**LIVE: RANGLEKLODS, (DK)
BASKETBALL (CA), SKIING (DE)**

+ SL REGULARS OH! MEHR!, MARI ME,
BEATHOVEN, LA CHRONICA AND
VJ LINARDS KULLES +

MAY 1, CHEZ JACKI

AN DER SCHILLING BRÜCKE

TERRACE OPEN FROM 18.00 - FREE
CLUB OPEN FROM 22.00
€5 BEFORE 24.00, €6 AFTER

WESTGERMANY

Handsome Furs
Basketball
S/L (DJ)

Kevin Halpin

shameless limitless presents...
handsome
furs
[sub pop]
basketball
[can]
may 9
westgermany
DOORS: 21:00 SHOW: 22:00
SKALITZER STR. 133 U1/8 KOTTBUSSER TOR

Kool Thing
Blackbird Blackbird
Mari Me (DJ)
Bokonon (DJ)
Detlev D. Saaster (DJ)
Linards Kulless (VJ)
David Addison (Live Painting)

Zille Sophie Bostinius

22. JULI 2011
SHAMELESS LIMITLESS
presents...

KOOL THING [Berlin]
BLACKBIRD BLACKBIRD [USA]

DJs MARI ME / BOKONON /
DETLEV D. SAASTER (Bauzugrecords)

Video Installation by LINARDS KULLESS

NAHERHOLUNG STERNCHEN
OPENING EVENT

Berolina Straße 7, U5 Schillingstraße

22:00 / 5€

Hush Hush
DENA
Easton West (DJ)
Paulo (DJ)
Mino (DJ)
BOMT b2b Mari Me (DJ)
Dale Phurrough (Exhibiting Artist)
Tank (Exhibiting Artist)

Shameless/Limitless. Need we say more?
///
Live:
Hush Hush
Back from touring the USA with Yeasayer, Berlin-based soul / r&b
dance-hit-machine Hush Hush is here to make ze party sizzle.
Consider yourself warned.

D E N A
Currently recording her debut album at Kaiku Studios, D E N A falls
in a long and distinguished pop tradition of concerning oneself with,
inter alia, bad boyfriends, getting on the guest list and making our
collective socks hop. In other words, F U N.
///
Video Installation by Tank + Dale Phurrough
///
DJs:
Easton West (Son Of Cataclysm)
Paulo (Airdrop Records)
Mino (Osaka)
BOMT b2b Mari Me (S/L)
///
€5 at the door

David Addison

FRIDAY 16TH SEPTEMBER 2011

SHAMELESS / LIMITLESS

presents

LIVE ↰ **HUSH HUSH**
DENA ★ ★ ★

with DJS: EASTON WEST ★ PAULO
MINO ★ BOMT B2B MARI ME

VIDEO INSTALLATION BY: DALE PHURROUGH & TANK ★

at

NÄHERHOLUNG STERNCHEN
BEROLINASTRAßE 7 / U5 SCHILLINGSTRAßE

★ 22:00/5€ ★

2011 09 24   MINDPIRATES
                HANDSOME FURS AFTER PARTY

                Handsome Furs (DJ)
                Kool Thing (DJ)
                La Chronica (DJ)

Veronica Manchego

HANDSOME FURS
(SUB POP)

AFTER PARTY & DJ SET

WITH DJ SUPPORT FROM:
KOOL THING
LA CHRONICA

SEP 24 2011
23:00

MIND PIRATES
Falckensteinstraße 48
(Enter between Magnet & San Remo)
€3

SHAMELESS
/LIMITLESS

Yip Deceiver
DENA
Skiing
Oh! Mehr! (DJ)

Shameless/Limitless is happy to host the Berlin debut of Yip Deceiver
(featuring members from of Montreal), who combine experimental dance pop
with '80s R&B and new wave.
//
We is also well chuffed to have Berlin's new pop royalty, D E N A, back by
popular demand for another show.
//
Skiing will be celebrating the online release of their new EP. This will
be the band's fourth S/L party this year. One more and they will be
eligible to claim rewards from our loyalty program.
//
Oh and also — dance party late into the night with Oh! Mehr!
€5

Denitza Todorova

SHAMELESS LIMITLESS
presents:
YIP DECEIVER
LIVE!
featuring members from OF MONTREAL
Skiing
LIVE!
DANCE PARTY WITH DJ OH!MEHR!
&
DENA
LIVE!
21. OCTOBER 2011
BEROLINASTR. 7 // U5 SCHILLINGSTR.
NAHERHOLUNG STERNCHEN
23H // 5€

Babe Rainbow
Rangleklods
Butterclock
Bokonon (DJ)
Mino (DJ)
Rafael Finns (DJ)
Yuki (Exhibiting Artist)

Wenn schon denn schon. I mean, this is a celebration of our 3rd birthday,
so why not? To hyperbolize the excellence of what's on tap is challenging
to say the least.
//
Live:
Babe Rainbow (WARP / Vancouver)
Babe Rainbow aka Cam Reed is many things. Vancouver scene lynchpin.
Over at his tumblr, arbiter of internet finery. Above all, though,
he is the creator of righteous off kilter electronic soundscapes.
This, his first European tour, finds him sharing stages with Battles,
Metronomy, Oneohtrix Point Never and AraabMuzik.

Rangleklods (Aarhus / Copenhagen)
Perennial S/L favourite is back in Berlin after a too-long absence. Since
last gracing a local stage, Rangleklods has toured Denmark extensively and
recently celebrated the official release of his debut EP, Home. We are
thrilled to have him back.

Butterclock (Paris / Berlin) CANCELLED
//
Performative installation by Japanese artist Yuki in the gallery.
//
Also, of course, tanz fest galore with DJs
Bokonon (S/L)
Mino (Osaka)
Rafael Finns (E´de Cologne)
//
New and improved bar design courtesy of Linards Kulless
//
€5 before 24:00, €7 after

David Addison

Teengirl Fantasy
Butterclock
Green Flash (DJ)

Today is a lucky one for you, as today is the day you are personally
invited to partake in the glory that will be Teengirl Fantasy (R&S
Records, USA) and Butterclock (Paris / Berlin) playing live at Naherholung
Sternchen on Feb 1. First ever Green Flash (which consists of two S/L
regulars) DJ set too? Ay, caramba! It's all coming true!

Proudly presented by Shameless/Limitless.

Tickets at the door.
Doors 21:00, Show 22:00

Find Naherholung Sternchen behind Kino International / Rathaus Mitte,
U5 Schillingstraße. 10-minute walk from Jannowitzbrücke or Alexanderplatz.

Evita Vasiļjeva & Joakim Drescher

SHAMELESS
LIMITLESS
presents

FEB 1ST, 2012

TEENGIRL
FANTASY

BUTTERCLOCK

+
GREEN FLASH
DJ SET

NAHERHOLUNG STERNCHEN

BEROLINASTRAßE 7   DOORS 21:00

/ U5 SCHILLINGSTRAßE   SHOW 22:00

MARIE-ANTOINETTE

        Gauntlet Hair
        Skiing
        S/L (DJ)

SATURDAY
FEBRUARY 25

SHAMELESS
LIMITLESS

presents

GAUNTLET
HAIR
(DEAD OCEANS / USA)

Skiing
(Berlin)

MARIE ANTOINETTE
HOLZMARKTSTRASSE 15-18
AN DER MICHAELBRÜCKE
U8 JANNOWITZBRÜCKE
DOORS 21:00 SHOW 22:00

CHRISTOPHER KLINE
Designer
Early Labyrinth
Hush Hush

With the hopes of riches and stardom
dashed on the existential rocks of the internet age,
the addicts still swarm among the ruins
littered with old easyJet boarding passes,
gas station receipts,
and triple-digit YouTube views
in search of that old fix:
the sweaty basements and backrooms of youth
when music made you feel new.

Enter Shameless/Limitless …
a glimmer of unflinching optimism
amid a scene of scrounging international transplants:
musicians and dilettantes
creating in scattered balls
of self-imposed solo projects
after bands became another unsustainable victim
of late-capitalist austerity
or the century of the Self
or both.

While still not yet certain whether S/L is a veritable astronomer
(charting the stars, assembling constellations)
or a hack astrologer
beckoning us into their velvety lair
via pasted posters along one's trudge
through the wet and cobbled Neukölln streets
pretending to read the future
in a random shuffle of drink tickets
one thing is clear:
the glass ceiling of Berlin
probably can't be cracked

but maybe it's better that way
so the future lies in the hands
of those who collect the pfand

MARIE-ANTOINETTE

Handsome Furs
Basketball
CANCELLED

NAHERHOLUNG STERNCHEN

Teen Daze
Brothertiger
Mari Me (DJ)
S/L (DJ)

SHAMELESS / LIMITLESS

PRESENTS...

TEEN DAZE CAN

BROTHERTIGER USA

DJs MARI ME AND S/L

APRIL 27/ DOORS 23:00

NAHERHOLUNG STERNCHEN

BEROLINASTRAßE 7/U5 SCHILLINGSTRAßE

NAHERHOLUNG STERNCHEN

Born Gold
Kuhrye-oo
No Fear Of Pop (DJ)

NO FEAR OF POP

NO FEAR OF POP
& SHAMELESS LIMITLESS
PRESENT

BORN GOLD CA

FORMERLY GOBBLE GOBBLE

kuhrye-oo CA

DJ: NO FEAR OF POP

MAY 16, 9PM
NAHERHOLUNG STERNCHEN
-> U5 SCHILLINGSTRAßE
nofearofpop.net / spoontrain.no

SHAMELESS LIMITLESS

Yip Deceiver
Hush Hush
S/L (DJ)

After presenting their super fun debut European show in October 2011,
Shameless/Limitless is happy to welcome back of Montreal side project Yip
Deceiver for a concert at the much hallowed WestGermany.

Yip Deceiver play an engaging, playful take on '80s R&B, new wave and
electro, with hooks big enough to lure a barracuda or sea bass or whatever
your favourite musical fish is. Their captivating, upbeat live show
elicits chortles of glee ranging from "Holy hell this is fun" to "Gosh I'm
glad this is happening right now and that I am here." Think Chromeo drunk
on Kool-Aid and Prince and you're halfway there. They are currently in the
midst of an extensive European tour. Don't sleep!

For extra incentive, the louche, infamous, fan favourite Berlin-based
R&B Dance Hit Machine HUSH HUSH will open.

SHAMELESS
LIMITLESS
PRESENTS...

17.05.2012

YIZ
DECEIVER
Members from
of Montreal

R'n'B Smash Hit Machine
Hush Hush

WestGermany
Skalitzerstr 133
Kottbusser Tor
21:00

Blackbird Blackbird
Molly Nilsson

Shameless/Limitless feels a whole thesaurus's worth of synonyms for
excellent about presenting BLACKBIRD BLACKBIRD (who played a particularly
good set at an S/L party last July) and MOLLY NILSSON (the undisputed
queen of Berlin DIY pop) for a show at the ever-evolving, always excellent
Naherholung Sternchen.

Vanessa Khoury

SHAMELESS / LIMITLESS

presents

BLACKBIRD BLACKBIRD

MOLLY NILSSON

Naherholung Sternchen
Berolinastraße 7 / U5 Schillingstraße
21:00

21/05/2012

2012 05 23   DAS GIFT
                    MOONFACE & SIINAI AFTER PARTY

                    Moonface (DJ)
                    Oh! Mehr! (DJ)

Viviane Chil-Hagopian

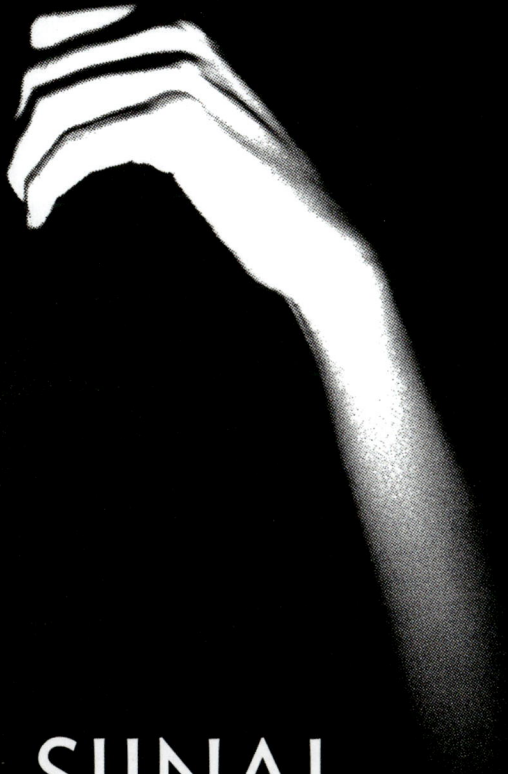

SHAMELESS / LIMITLESS

PRESENTS

MOONFACE

SIINAI

AFTER PARTY & DJ SET

23.05.12
DAS GIFT, DONAUSTRAßE 119

Teengirl Fantasy
Fatima Al Qadiri (DJ)
Joey Hansom (DJ)
Clay Hooves
S/L (DJ)

Good god this one came together in about as major a way as is possible.
Teengirl Fantasy back at Shameless/Limitless and playing new tracks from
their much-hyped sophomore record? The Berlin debut and exclusive German
show of the indomitable, rarely seen and hugely sought-after Fatima
Al Qadiri? Joey Hansom's DJing prowess? And Clay Hooves too? A little
largesse never hurt anyone, so come join us in revelling royally in this
bounty of party excellence.

Teengirl Fantasy (R&S Records, Brooklyn)
Shameless/Limitless is thrilled to welcome back Teengirl Fantasy, who are
touring in advance of their soon-to-be released sophomore record, Tracer.
The LP, which will be the group's debut for the much-hallowed R&S records,
features guest vocals from Panda Bear, Romanthony, Laurel Halo and more.
Looking back, the duo were responsible for the instant club classic (and
FACT Magazine's favourite track of 2010) Cheaters, from their uniformly
well received debut, 7AM.

Fatima Al Qadiri (Tri Angle, Brooklyn)
Based in New York, but born in Senegal and raised in Kuwait, renowned
multimedia artist and musician Fatima Al Qadiri has been around. That
said, she doesn't get around — she rarely plays out outside of New York.
And so, this, her Berlin debut and one of only two European shows, is
something very special, if not wholly unbelievable.

Clay Hooves (Berlin)
Clay Hooves is an electronic musician who hails from Edinburgh and is
currently based in Berlin. After 10 years of playing and touring with
bands with various post suffixes, he endeavoured to work on his own on
electronic music in the summer of 2011 in Brooklyn, NY. Since moving
to Berlin in late 2011, Clay Hooves has further finessed his sound and
is now prepared to set it free. This party will mark his Berlin debut.

Viviane Chil-Hagopian

SHAMELESS / LIMITLESS

PRESENTS

R&S RECORDS, NYC

TEENGIRL FANTASY

TRI ANGLE, NYC

FATIMA AL QADIRI

FRIDAY 20TH JULY 23:00

NAHERHOLUNG STERNCHEN / BEROLINASTRAßE 7

U5 Schillingstraße. U8 Jannowitzbrücke

Dear Facebook user,

You are warmly invited to Neukölln's friendliest bar — Das Gift — this
Wednesday night, for an after party and DJ set with Brian and Dave, aka
the two nice guys who make up the awesome, hugely acclaimed Vancouver-
based band JAPANDROIDS. It will be a night of wine and roses, young hearts
sparking fires, and celebration rock.

Your boyfriend and ours, Berlin-based artist Justin Frederick will warm up
the excitable early birds with a cross section of his preferred jams.

Like all things at DG, this event is free and open to all. Gleefully
presented by Shameless/Limitless.

Kevin Halpin

2012 09 26   DAS GIFT
                    DIRTY BEACHES AFTER PARTY

                    Dirty Beaches (DJ)
                    Oh! Mehr! (DJ)

Following their show at WestGermany, Alex Hungtai and the good lads of
Berlin's favourite lo-fi crooner ensemble Dirty Beaches (Montreal) will
head over to Das Gift to DJ and to drink.

S/L alum and good friend Oh! Mehr! will kick things off around 10 bells
doing what he does best. Worth coming early for, no doubt.

Free entry, as always. Seems like a foolproof plan to me.

Justin Worhaug

DIRTY BEACHES

SHAMELESS /LIMITLESS

PRESENTS...

DIRTY BEACHES
AFTER PARTY & DJ SET
DAS GIFT
DONAUSTRAßE 119
26/09/12

TOPS
Dan Bodan
Touchy Mob
Pissypaw (DJ)
S/L (DJ)

Noisekölln and Shameless/Limitless present the Berlin debut of TOPS
(Arbutus, Montreal). Also — the ever-charming Dan Bodan (DFA / MMW1, Berlin)
and the always winning Touchy Mob (Berlin). DJs also because of course.
The show is happening at Freudenreich Berlin, a sweet new venue located
at Sonnenallee 67. Party on.

Carmen Paula Negrelli

Noiseköln & Shameless // Limitless
present
TOPS
DAN BODAN (DFA)
TOUCHY MOB (BERLIN)
+ DJs!!!...
Saturday, November 3, 2012
Freudenreich Berlin
Sonnenalle 67
23:00
(ARBUTUS... ...MONTREAL)

JANE PENNY
TOPS

In 2012 I went on my first-ever European tour with my band TOPS. We did the entire tour via Megabus, a discount intercity passenger bus service. We carried our instruments on our backs with special instrument backpacks and wheeled our suitcases from station to station. After countless empty rooms and long bus rides spent catching up on sleep by laying across the only empty rows of seats (often directly across from the toilet), we made it to Berlin. And in Berlin we played the only show on the entire tour that was well attended, a party thrown by Shameless/Limitless.

The show was in a basement venue with a backstage moonlighting as some random dealer's accounting department. And to our surprise, there was an actual audience waiting for us in that sweaty dungeon. A fun audience. Old friends and new dancing and cheering us on. It was the first time that I was able to glimpse a future where we might be embraced outside of our hometown, Montreal. Now that I'm living in Berlin, I get to attend a lot of these "first real shows", to see the first time a musician gets to play to a full room in a small to mid-sized venue. They're some of my favourite nights out. And nine times out of ten they're brought to you by Shameless/Limitless.

2012 11 14   MONARCH
                 PURITY RING AFTER PARTY

                 Blood Diamonds (DJ)
                 Doldrums (DJ)
                 Clay Hooves (DJ)

Linda Mai Green

SHAMELESS
LIMITLESS

PRESENTS
PURITY RING AFTER PARTY

WITH DJ SETS FROM
DOLDRUMS
BLOOD DIAMONDS
CLAY HOOVES

14.11.2012
MONARCH
SKALITZERSTR. 134

Mac DeMarco
Each Other
Puschenrealgood (DJ)
S/L (DJ)

Puschen and Shameless/Limitless are thoroughly pleased to present
Sunday Fun Day, an afternoon extravaganza with the Berlin debut of
one of the most exciting new artists of the year, Mac DeMarco. Having
previously fronted the lo-fi favourites that were Makeout Videotape,
DeMarco now prolifically writes laid-back, good-time garage pop jams in
the vein of Ram-era Paul McCartney. His new record, 2, (Captured Tracks)
was released to stellar reviews (Best New Music!) on October 16.

Each Other (like Mac, from Montreal) keep it messy, lo-fi and loud.
In other words, excellent. This will be their Berlin debut.

Gaia Che — aka Gai's Fruitcake — will be on hand to sell a variety
of home baked tasty treats. Come get 'em while they're hot.

Music before, between and after sets provided by — you guessed it —
DJs Puschenrealgood and S/L.

David Addison

PUSCHEN & SHAMELESS LIMITLESS PRESENT...

• NOVEMBER 25TH 2012 •

SUNDAY FUNDAY
AN AFTERNOON EXTRAVAGANZA
WITH

MAC DEMARCO
(CAPTURED TRACKS, MONTREAL)

EACH OTHER MONTREAL

PLUS: DJs BAKED GOODS GOOD TIMES

at MONARCH

DOORS 4:00 SHOW 5:00 • SKALITZER STR 134

TICKETS AT KOKA 36

Nü Sensae
Ruins of Krüger
Frank Freshness (DJ)

Paper and Iron, Eine Welt Aus Hack and Shameless/Limitless proudly
present the Berlin debut of no fun city punk champions Nü Sensae at the
hallowed halls of WestGermany. Support comes courtesy of local no wave
upstarts Ruins of Krüger. Tickets at the door.

NÜ (CAN)
SENSAE

18/4/2013
HAFENKLANG
HAMBURG

20/4/2013
WESTGERMANY
BERLIN

AUFTOUREN.DE · Byte™ · OX · noisey

eine Zeit aus Pech · SHAMELESS/LIMITLESS · PAPERANDIRONBOOKING.COM

2013 04 22   NAHERHOLUNG STERNCHEN

                    Autre Ne Veut
                    18+
                    S/L (DJ)

Anton Benois

SHAMELESS
/ LIMITLESS

PRESENTS

AUTRE NE VEUT
(MEXICAN SUMMER/SOFTWARE, NYC)

+ SPECIAL GUESTS
————————

APRIL 22, 2013 / 21:00

NAHERHOLUNG STERNCHEN

BEROLINASTRASSE 7 : U5 SCHILLINGSTRASSE / U8 JANNOWITZBRÜCKE

Co La
Conquering Animal Sound
Touchy Mob (DJ)

Ieva Kraule

PAPER AND IRON BOOKING
AND SHAMELESS/LIMITLESS PRESENT...

CO LA
(SOFTWARE / MEXICAN SUMMER, USA)

CONQUERING ANIMAL SOUND (UK)

TOUCHY MOB (BERLIN) DJ SET

06/05/13

21:00/URBAN SPREE/REVALER STR. 99

Tonstartssbandht
A Tribe Called Red
Half Girl / Half Sick (DJ)
DJ Brot

Noisekölln and Shameless/Limitless, together again, presenting:
Tonstartssbandht (Arbutus, Montreal), A Tribe Called Red (Ottawa),
Half Girl / Half Sick (Berlin) and DJ Brot (Berlin).

Tonstartssbandht are two brothers who enjoy pairing "freak" and "far"
with "out". Signed to the very hot Arbutus Records, they are in the midst
of an insane tour around Europe including a handful of shows in Russia
with Dirty Beaches.

Ottawa's A Tribe Called Red are a Native American DJ crew who mix
traditional Pow Wow music with club magic. In other words, they're doing
something new with something old and they're doing it fantastically.
They will be making their Berlin debut and celebrating the release of
their new record, which drops May 7th.

Half Girl / Half Sick is one half of Berlin bass music club institution
Sick Girls.

Thursday is a holiday — stay late!

L. Zylberberg

City Dragon
Moon Wheel
SFTSTPS
Sisters of Seance
Hyaenas (DJ)

Shameless/Limitless presents the Berlin debuts of saxophone god loop
experimentalist City Dragon (Villa Villa Nola, Paris) + Sisters of
Seance (Toronto), the Persian drone audio / visual project of Luke Rogers,
from noted pan global maximalists (and Shameless/Limitless favourites)
Basketball.

Also on the bill is Moon Wheel (Berlin via Sweden), whose new record just
came out on much-loved label Not Not Fun.

Just back from shows in Morocco and beyond, critical theory Ph.D. candidate
and pop cut up artist extraordinaire SFTSTPS is based in Berlin but has
a pedigree extending far and wide, including stints as part of the noted
Rhinoceropolis collective in Denver.

Finally, Hyaenas will spin desert and sub-Saharan jams until the sun
comes up.

Nicholas Houde

Scan 6.jpeg @ 16.7% (City Dragon (Villa Villa Nola, Paris) Moon Wheel (Not Not Fun, , RGB/8*) *
Scan 2.jpeg @ 16.7% (RGB/8*)
Scan 6.jpeg @ 16.7% (City Dragon (Villa Villa Nola, Paris) Moon Wheel (Not Not Fun, , RGB/8*) *
shameless
/limitless/
presents
shameless
/limitless/
presents
shameless
/limitless/
presents
shameless
/limitless/
presents
City Dragon (Villa
Moon Wheel (Not
SFTSTPS (Berlin)
Sisters of Seance
+
DJs
Hyaenas
S/L
25/05/13
Loophole
Boddinstr 60
U7 Rathaus Ne
16.67%
Doc: 24.1M/24.1M

Slow Magic
Giraffage
Mister Lies
Rejections
DJ Richard
JR Seaton (DJ)
Alienata (DJ)
Rodeo
Clay Hooves
DJ Brot
Michael Aniser (DJ)
S/L (DJ)

Certain endeavours require a higher order of celebration. A celebration that defies not only expectations, but also assumptions and notions of just what a party is and is capable of achieving. Celebrations that burn white hot impressions onto the fabric of our very existence as we journey ever onwards, grasping at the moments and events that reinforce the glory of existence.

Not sure if the pairing of Shameless/Limitless and NO for a Friday night at the end of May requires that manner of celebration, but we're going for it anyways!

BEHOLD:

S/L takes over upstairs, with LIVE sets from:
Slow Magic (USA)
Giraffage (USA)
Mister Lies (Lefse, USA) *Berlin debut!*
Rodeo (Berlin)
Clay Hooves (Berlin)

NO #3 tends to matters below in the MASTURBASEMENT with this stunner of a lineup:

Rejections *live*
(Opal Tapes / Reject and Fade)
First time in Berlin! Rejections is pushing the boundaries of straight up harsh noise and industrial towards a new kind of iridescent sound.

DJ Richard (White Material Records)
Alienata (Kat Channel / Snuff Traxx)
JR Seaton (Call Super inc.)
DJ Brot (NO / Moon Wheel)
Michael Aniser (Mr Noisekölln himself)

Victoria Gisborne-Land

Shameless/Limitless x Noisekölln

ॐ

May 31, 2013

SLOW MAGIC | GIRAFFAGE | MISTER LIES

RODEO | CLAY HOOVES | S/L

NO #3: Masturbasement

REJECTIONS
LIVE
(OPAL TAPES/REJECT AND FADE)

DJ RICHARD | ALIENATA | JR SEATON

DJ BROT | MICHAEL ANISER

Naherholung Sternchen
Berolinastraße 7, U5 Schillingstraße / U8 Jannowitzbrücke

Terror Bird
Pacific Strings
Mattress
unhappybirthday

Shameless/Limitless proudly presents a 4-band extravaganza on a warm
summer's night in the shadow of the TV Tower, featuring the return of glam
pop champions Terror Bird (Vancouver), Berlin-based jangle pop favourites
Pacific Strings, the Berlin debut of Portland's weirdo king Mattress, and
Wismar's reigning heartthrobs unhappybirthday.

Daniela Roessler

SHAMELESS
/ LIMITLESS

presents

TERROR
BIRD
(VANCOUVER)

UNHAPPY
BIRTHDAY
(WISMAR)

PACIFIC
STRINGS
(BERLIN)

MATTRESS
(PORTLAND)

JUNE 5, 2013
NAHERHOLUNG STERNCHEN
BEROLINASTRAßE 7
U5 SCHILLINGSTRAßE / U8 JANNOWITZBRÜCKE
20:00

ERIC HALPIN
Shameless/Limitless Co-founder

Now 12 years in, and after
thousands of email threads,
plenty of ups and some downs, an
unwavering determination and
DIY ethos, strong support from
friends and family, gallons
of free shots of mexicaner w/
purchase of beer, a multitude
of kilometres walked to paste
posters on the streets, and
ultimately an abundance of
concerts, parties and bar
hangs that have made for oh
so many unforgettable nights,
there's no doubt that Kevin is
the majority shareholder in
Shameless/Limitless Limited.

Molly Nilsson
Dylan III
Julie Chance (DJ)
S/L (DJ)

DARK SKIES ASSOCIATION and SHAMELESS/LIMITLESS proudly present the launch
party for Molly Nilsson's upcoming album The Travels.

NOTE NEW VENUE — The show will now happen at Berghain.

Tickets cost €8 and will be available at the door.

MOLLY NILSSON

The Travels

Album Release Show and Party

19/06/2013
20:00 uhr

Molly Nilsson - Live
Dylan III - Live
DJs – Shameless/Limitless and Julie Chance
(Kool Thing)

BERGHAIN

70 Am Wriezener Bahnhof

SHAMELESS
/LIMITLESS

DARK
SKIES
ASSOCIATION

Cold Cave
Pale Male

Molly Nilsson
ManMachine
Telepathe (DJ)

Farewell. Bon Voyage. Sayonara.

In anticipation of Molly Nilsson's impending North American tour and
travels, a celebration has been slated in which Molly + friends will play
live at the newly renovated and expanded Naherholung Sternchen. Freshly
pressed and shipped vinyl copies of Molly's newest record, The Travels,
will also be available for purchase, which is a cause for celebration in
and of itself. So, come bid adieu and adios, aloha and see you later,
at least for now.

ManMachine will be making a special (now EU-approved!) trip from Zagreb
for his Berlin debut in the support slot. Simply put, Goran Uroich, in
the guise of ManMachine, delivers emotional and life-changing performances
of meaningful songs ripe with timeless melodies, utilizing only a
keyboard, a microphone and his own genius.

(Short-term) departures make way for arrivals, and so we are more than
happy to have Melissa Livaudais (who recently relocated to Berlin) of
celebrated pop experi-mentalists Telepathe (Federal Prism) tending to
DJ matters.

Tickets will be available at the door only.

Kate Mackeson

Safe Travels
Molly Nilsson

14.08.13
20:30

+ManMachine (Zagreb)
Telepathe (DJ)

DARK
SKIES
ASSOCIATION

Naherholung Sternchen, Berolinastraße 7
U5 Schillingstraße / U8 Jannowitzbrücke

SHAMELESS
LIMITLESS

Blue Hawaii (DJ)
Oh! Mehr! (DJ)
DJ Brot
S/L (DJ)

Shameless/Limitless and Sameheads, together at last.

Please do come and join us for a pairing that feels like it has been
years in the making.

There will be carousing a-plenty, with a lineup that includes DJ sets
from Alex of AGOR / Blue Hawaii (Arbutus, Montreal), the return of S/L
favourite and O.G. Oh! Mehr!, and righteous tunage courtesy of DJ BROT.
Friendly price for all — this is, after all, a celebration.

Andréas Thorstensson

14/09/13

Shameless Limitless presents:

Blue Hawaii DJ (Arbutus, Montreal)

Oh! Mehr!

DJ Brot

S/L

Sameheads
Richardstr 10.
23:00

SHAMELESS /LIMITLESS

Artwork: Andréas Thorstensson

Skiing
Beliefs
Caroline Clifford (Stand-up)

Started from the bottom now we're here. Or, more accurately, back.
Well actually, I guess we kind of started at the top, as playing
WestGermany is really kind of a peak. So, started at the top and now
we're still here, but now better than ever.

What I'm saying is this: since S/L hosted Skiing's first-ever show, at
WestGermany in Jan 2011, the band has released 1 EP and 2 LPs, the most
recent of which, Holly, is a strong contender for record of the year.
This show will mark the band's return to where it all began.

Beliefs, champions of fuzzed out shoegaze dream pop, are a Toronto-
based band who are in the midst of their first European tour. Slots at
the Incubate and Reeperbahn festivals and choice pull quotes from The
Guardian, Dazed & Confused and Noisey suggest that they are on
a trajectory similar to that of their more famous fellow Torontonian
quoted above.

Also, for something different, Caroline Clifford will be doing a
hilarious set of stand-up between bands, as she is hilarious and
that is what she does. We got the whole team here!

Joel Alas

Shameless/Limitless
presents:

SKIING

The band
Aus Berlin

Plus special guests

BELIEFS Toronto
(No Pain In Pop)

And comedy by

CAROLINE CLIFFORD

Performing at

WESTGERMANY

Skalitzer Str. 133, Kottbusser Tor

26/09/2013 - 21:00

Sean Nicholas Savage
Small Black
Blue Hawaii (DJ)
Touchy Mob (DJ)

PUSCHEN
& SHAMELESS LIMITLESS
PRESENT

FRIDAY 4TH OCTOBER 2013

SMALL BLACK
(JAGJAGUWAR)

SEAN NICHOLAS SAVAGE (ARBUTUS)

BLUE HAWAII DJ SET
(ARBUTUS)

DOORS OPEN 21.00

TOUCHY MOB DJ SET

AT KANTINE AM BERGHAIN

TICKETS FROM KOKA 36

Phèdre
SFTSTPS
Cape

Shameless/Limitless proudly presents Toronto's honey hero weirdos
Phèdre + no barrier fun DIY-hard pop pastiche specialist SFTSTPS and
Berlin's Bauhaus champions, 케이프 (aka CAPE).

If Phèdre's videos are any indication, things could get weird.

SFTSTPS. Yippee ki-yay — this is your lucky night. Come on feel the vibes.

케이프 (CAPE) apply Bauhaus to pop music. They just released their 3rd ep.

Tickets available at the door only. How much do you think they will cost?
Yeah, you're pretty much right.

Kate Mackeson

10/10/13

Shameless / Limitless Presents

Phèdre

(DAPS, Toronto)

&

SFTSTPS (Berlin)

Cape (Berlin)

Naherholung Sternchen
Berolinastraße 7
U5 Schillingstraße/U8 Jannowitzbrücke

21:00

Touchy Mob (DJ)
Vero Manchego (DJ)
Dreea (DJ)
S/L (DJ)
Kandis Williams (DJ, Cancelled)

Round 1 with Sameheads back in September was so much fun that I figure
that they and I would both be remiss in our duties as party starters and
fun-time makers if we didn't give an encore a shot.

What an encore it is, with DJ sets from Touchy Mob (who is rapidly
ascending to music bro # 1, both in the confines of the 'hood and the
greater world at large), old friend, original S/L co-conspirator and
Neukölln overlord Vero Manchego, and renowned dance floor firebrand and
upstanding community organizer Dreea.

Entry will be cheap as chips, and vibes will be festive to the Nth.

❤️HB *JK* ❤️

Au revoir, Sophie G x

Evita Vasiļjeva

SHAMELESS
/LIMITLESS

presents...
PARTY TIME
with DJ sets from:

TOUCHY MOB
KANDIS WILLIAMS
VERONICA MANCHEGO

25/10/2013
23:00
SAMEHEADS
RICHARDSTR.10

Molly Nilsson
Beaver Sheppard

On Nov 6, please join us at Shift for a homecoming, an introduction, and a celebration of Going Places, with live performances from:

Molly Nilsson (Berlin, Dark Skies Association)
Beaver Sheppard (No Weapon, Montreal)

Times were had, sights were seen, drinks were drunk and friends were made. Road trips of herculean proportions anticipated, endured and conquered. All manner of ideas and experiences contemplated, approved, executed — except for the ones that weren't. Late nights and later mornings, and days that didn't seem to end. Two months, three countries and a whole host of memorable shows later, Molly Nilsson is back from her travels, but still as excited as ever to keep going places.

One of those friends who was met along the way is Beaver Sheppard, a renaissance man, certified big hat chef and tireless songwriter who doubles as one of Montreal's top-tier party personalities. Recommended listening.

GOING PLACES

MOLLY NILSSON (Live)

BEAVER SHEPPARD (Live)

SHIFT

6.NOVEMBER 2010 21:00
Köpenickerstr.70 Berlin
SHAMELESS/LIMITLESS
DARKSKIESASSOCIATION

MAX KAARIO
City Dragon
cmptrmthmtcs

Shameless/Limitless has been a presence on my horizon of event serie
since before I began organizing cmptrmthmtcs in Paris sometime i
2012. A fresh transplant to Paris, at that point the awareness o
ny other event series in Europe was a source of energy for my ow
magined event productions, and S/L offered a convincing face to
that was possible.

The event organization of most forms of performance which do no
ely on government or private funding must forge a community whic
repeats its adherence through the strategic creation of a particula
rban atmosphere, and I knew that Kevin had done just that whe
I attended my first Shameless/Limitless event as a performer in
May 2013. From that experience I gathered that S/L events offe
a collective result that bends beyond the limitations of simple
money-making ends achieved through the fetishization of cool music

But I have to admit, that despite my desire to detract from the
mportance of music quality at an event, I am a keen and constant
listener of whatever music program Shameless/Limitless is cooking
though I am far away in Paris, when Kevin posts an event, I liste
carefully to the artists being presented. Our boy has a knac
to dig up gold, and I consider myself lucky that S/L has sen
over multiple artists to play cmptrmthmtcs shows in Paris ove
the years.

However, let me get to the point. More than anything, over time
our international exchange of taste and talk, Berlin-Paris
Paris-Berlin, has for me best been crystalized in walks around
centres of urban energy, often with tall cans of beer in hand
late at night or early in the afternoon, strolling the Butte
Chaumont or Tempelhofer Feld with a belief that the city street
has a salubrious potential to heal and ignite. Discussions abou
events: mutual understanding of the poetics of logistics; a sincere
engagement with the aesthetics of lounge; an idea of responsibility
that admits the complexity of organizing events in a gentrifying
urban neighbourhood … These off-site dialogues, away from an
actual event, have made the difference for me between the pretence
of professional encounter and the breaching of friendship in

2013 11 09   TEAM TITANIC

Gary War
Purple Pilgrims

Mihkel Maripuu

November 9th 2013

SHAMELESS LIMITLESS

GARY WAR (usa)
PURPLE PiLGRiMS
(New Zealand)

@TEAM TITANIC
FLUGHAFFENSTR. 50
U8 Boddinstraße
21:00Uhr

MONARCH

Dent May
Slow Steve

NOVEMBER 10TH 2013

PUSCHEN & SHAMELESS LIMITLESS

present

SUNDAY FUNDAY PART 2

AN AFTERNOON EXTRAVAGANZA

with

DENT MAY

PAW TRACKS–USA

and

SLOW STEVE

BERLIN

DJS   MASSAGES   BAKED GOODS   GOOD TIMES

plus

at

MONARCH

SKALITZER STR 134

DOORS: 4PM   SHOW: 5PM

TICKETS FROM KOKA 36 & TICKETS.DE

No Joy
Secret Secret Girl
Doom Squad

NO JOY
(MEXICAN SUMMER, MONTREAL)

SECRET SECRET GIRL
(MONTREAL)

DOOM SQUAD
(HAND DRAWN DRACULA, TORONTO)

28/11/13
URBAN SPREE
REVALER STR. 99
21:00

```
2013 12 13        URBAN SPREE
                  5 YEARS SHAMELESS/LIMITLESS

                  Touchy Mob & Dylan III
                  Jaakko Eino Kalevi
                  Femminielli Noir
                  Matt Didemus (DJ)
                  Molly Nilsson (DJ)
                  Friendboy (DJ)
                  Moon Wheel (DJ)
                  Vero Manchego (DJ)
                  S/L (DJ)
```

Please join us tonight in celebrating five years of no barrier fun with
this two-floor corker of a do featuring …

Live:
TOUCHY MOB / DYLAN III SUPER SET (One-off dream team performance from local
favourites)

JAAKKO EINO KALEVI (Flown in from Helsinki especially for the night,
this will be Jaakko's first show in Berlin as a Domino Records recording
artist)

FEMMINIELLI NOIR (New project from Bernardino Femminielli, ex Dirty
Beaches, and Jesse Osborne-Lanthier, Noir)

DJs:
MATT DIDEMUS (JUNIOR BOYS)

MOLLY NILSSON (Dark Skies Association)

FRIENDBOY (Cocktail d'Amore Music)

MOON WHEEL (Not Not Fun)

VERO MANCHEGO (Neukölln after party don)

S/L

Tome Atilla Vidoši

5 YEARS
SHAMELESS / LIMITLESS

LIVE / TOUCHY MOB W/ DYLAN III AND BETTER PERSON
JAAKKO EINO KALEVI (DOMINO RECORDS)
FEMMINIELLI NOIR (MONTREAL)
DJS / MATT DIDEMUS (JUNIOR BOYS)
FRIENDBOY (COCKTAIL D'AMORE RECORDS)
MOLLY NILSSON (DARK SKIES ASSOC.)
VERO MANCHEGO
MOON WHEEL (NOT NOT FUN)
S/L

13.12.13
URBAN SPREE / REVALER STR 99 22:30

MONARCH

    Robyn Hitchcock
    Joel Alas

Since The Devil Is Gone I Mostly Feel Lonely
& Shameless/Limitless Present...

ROBYN
HITCHCOCK

(UK: YEP ROC RECORDS)
FIRST BERLIN SHOW IN 18 YEARS

SPECIAL GUEST:

JOEL ALAS

(BERLIN: EX SKIING)

MONARCH

SKALITZER STR. 134   U: KOTTBUSSER TOR

THURS MARCH 27, 2014

DOORS: 20:00

MARIE-ANTOINETTE

Skiing
Classic Muscle
Absolulu (DJ)
Soda Fabric (DJ)

Späti Palace & Shameless Limitless present

Skiing

CLASSIC MUSCLE

APRIL 5TH

at Marie Antoinette

SPLIT 7"
RELEASE
PARTY

DOORS 8.30PM | MARIE ANTOINETTE HOLZMARKT STR 15-17 | U8 JANNOWITZBRÜCKE
SPAETIPALACE.BANDCAMP.COM | SHAMELESSLIMITLESS.TUMBLR.COM

2014 04 06   URBAN SPREE
                  METRONOMY AFTER PARTY

                  Metronomy (DJ)
                  Luna Library (DJ)
                  Night Angles (DJ)
                  S/L (DJ)

Victoria Gisborne-Land

Keep It Together & Shameless/Limitless

Present...

THE OFFICIAL AFTER PARTY

METRONOMY

06.04.14

DJ sets from:

METRONOMY

NIGHT ANGLES

SHAMELESS/LIMITLESS

LUNA LIBRARY

22:30-End
Urban Spree, Revaler Straße 99
3/5 euros W/Without Ticket

Teen Daze
Magic Island
PONY

Shameless/Limitless warmly welcomes back one of the nicest (and most
musically versatile) dudes in the game, Teen Daze, for a headlining show
in support of his most recent LP, Glacier.

Support comes from Neukölln's one to watch for 2014, Magic Island, and the
debut performance from PONY.

As Naherholung Sternchen recently announced it will be closing at April's
end, this will mark the final S/L show there. Come get sentimental,
won't you?

Moritz Freudenberg

SHAMELESS
LIMITLESS

presents...

TEEN
DAZE

Abbotsford

MAGIC
ISLAND

Berlin

8th April
2014

20:30

Naherhohlung
Sternchen

PONY

Berlin

Berolinastr.7, 10178 Berlin

Molly Nilsson (DJ)
DENA (DJ)
Sean Nicholas Savage (DJ)
S/L (DJ)

Trumpet trumpet toot toot, I have an announcement to make: on the eve of
Friday, April 25, it is party time at the best place to have parties with
the funnest people to make parties. Plan accordingly.

DJ sets (and I hasten to highlight that these are all DJ sets — not live
shows) from now and forever Neukölln and beyond queen bee Molly Nilsson
(who recently returned to town after an extended stay living life right in
beautiful Buenos Aires), old-school S/L co-conspirator, current top of the
pops hit maker and undisputed flash fashion maven DENA, and a special set
from normcore torch bearer and continual zeitgeist definer, Sean Nicholas
Savage.

Also, S/L because of course.

Rest assured, entry is priced right and will be cheaper still for
the early birds.

Linda Mai Green

25.04.14

Shameless / Limitless
presents...

Party Time w/ DJs

MOLLY NILSSON
(Dark Skies Association, Berlin)

D E N A
(K7, Berlin)

SEAN NICHOLAS SAVAGE
(Arbutus, Montreal)

S/L

Sameheads
Richardstr. 10
22:30

MOLLY NILSSON
Artist
Designer

It was spring 2014, and I was set to DJ at an S/L party at Sameheads. I had accidentally started my weekend one day early and so I was already wrecked by Friday, the night of the party. My set was scheduled to start at 3 a.m. My hangover worsened by the hour, and so did the temperature and volume of the party. When I arrived, I didn't think I would even last an hour!

I remember standing in the makeshift coat check whining to Kevin like a drunk baby, about how I was so hungover I might actually die, begging to get fired and sent home on the spot. But of course he didn't fire me, or even listen. Instead he pressed two large drinks into my hands and gave me a moment to finish them. And just like that, miraculously, I rose from the undead and made my way down into the loud sweaty pit that is the basement of Sameheads.

The ceiling there is so low that you'd think you're wearing a hat, and the DJ booth is placed on one of those wooden pallets, preventing any sober person from safely standing there. The dancefloor is more like a carved-out hole, everything sort of pulling towards its centre.

I deejayed for about two hours, time which flew by. At 5 a.m. I was finishing my set and Sean Nicholas Savage, who I'd never met before, was about to take over. We shouted greetings over the music and I complimented him on his work, saying something like, I love your music, although I later had to admit I'd only heard two songs of his. We didn't talk any more that night and I can't recall what else happened, but it was a moment we would look back at and laugh about, years later, when we became a couple.

Torn Hawk
Dave I.D.
Cuticle
LX Sweat
Criese (DJ)

Shameless/Limitless proudly presents this incredibly stacked Saturday
night lineup with the live Berlin debuts of Torn Hawk (A/V), Cuticle and
LX Sweat. Dave I.D. makes his return after a much-vaunted performance
last year, and born and bred (and buttered) Berliner DJ Criese will ensure
that things end on a high note, crises resolved.

Finally, entry is cheap and totally affordable so don't you go stressing
about your €€€s.

10th May 2014

Torn Hawk
(L.I.E.S, Brooklyn) — Live

Dave I.D.
(MMWI/Federal Prism, London) — Live

Cuticle
(Not Not Fun, Iowa City) — Live

LX Sweat
(Not Not Fun, Germany) — Live

Criese
(Berlin) — DJ

OHM
(formerly Shift)
Köpenicker Straße 70
23:00

SHAMELESS
★ LIMITLESS ★

2014 05 15   WESTGERMANY

Group Rhoda
Dubais

Arita Varžinska & Atis Jākobsons

15/05/14

SHAMELESS/LIMITLESS PRESENTS

GROUP RHODA
(NOT NOT FUN / SAN FRANCISCO)

DUBAIS
(PORTLAND)

WEST GERMANY
SKALITZER STRASSE 133
21:00

SHAMELESS
/LIMITLESS

Doomsquad
Alex Cameron
PONY

Thursday night is thrice as nice when you've got shaman beat trailblazers Doomsquad, crooner deluxe Alex Cameron and dream weavers PONY to keep you in good company. That said, they say that three is a party, so who knows where this night is going to go …

Alex Cameron rolls hard and he rolls deep. He writes what he knows, he knows what he lives, and he lives fully completely. Berlin is richer for having Mr Cameron (who also fronts Sydney-based band Seekae) call it home for this all too fleeting period. All caps recommended, all caps 100% S/L endorsement, all caps capital A.

PONY consists of the nicest classically trained virtuoso brainiacs you have ever met. They play dark droney dream pop.

Frances Enyedy

:22/05/14:

SHAMELESS! PRESENTS.
LIMITLESS

DOOMSQUAD
(NO PAIN IN POP, TORONTO)

+

ALEX CAMERON
(SYDNEY)

+

PONY
(BERLIN)

@

MONARCH SKALITZER
STRAßE
134

20:00

SHAMELESS
/LIMITLESS

Phèdre
Rodeo

Shameless/Limitless warmly welcomes back Toronto's favourite rabble-
rousers Phèdre for the Berlin instalment of their trans-continental 3rd
Lyfe tour, with support from pop purist and proud parent of a brand-new
LP, Rodeo.

Smart money says that this show will be some form of a perfect
distillation of hot / summer / fun / woohoo / high five, so if any of these
concepts appeal to you, either in theory, in practice, or both, count
yourself as part the target demographic and therefore ideally
suited for participation.

Natalia Portnoy

SHAMELESS
LIMITLESS
11 / 06 / 14
PHÈDRE
(DAPS, Toronto)
RODEO
(Berlin)
Monarch
Skalitzer Str. 134
21:00

Mathematique
Magic Island
Jack Chosef
Better Person (DJ)
Jayyce (DJ)

Summer Cool Music and Shameless/Limitless have teamed up to bring you,
the ever-discerning concertgoer and wild cat party animal, a soiree to
satiate your longing to behold the best that Montreal and Berlin have
to offer.

Entry is cheap like always, no stre$$.

Summer Cool and Shameless/Limitless present

Mathematique (Montreal)

Magic Island (Berlin)

Jack Chosef (Berlin)

DJs Jayyce & Better Person
Loophole - Boddinstrasse 60
June 13th 2014 - 22:00

SHAMELESS
/LIMITLESS

Dylan III
Alex Cameron

Rare is the occasion, and yet, here it is.

Here we are.

You, there, looking on in wonder and amazement. That feeling is called contentment — hold on to it with every ounce you've got.

They, there, on the stage, doing the things that got them there in the first place, except this time better than ever.

Us, together, and all the better for it.

Shameless/Limitless enthusiastically presents an evening with motivational truth-sayer, accomplished pianist and celebrated man about town Dylan III. New on the block and all the rip-roaring better for it, show-stopper Alex Cameron (of Sydney's Seekae) will also be present, treating us to a full length set on this, the last of his Berlin engagements for the foreseeable future.

Take heed: this one comes highly recommended and is priced real nice.

Rhianne McNally

AIMLESS/ SHAMELESS/ WITLESS PRESENTS AN EVENING WITH

DYLAN III (BERLIN)
ALEX CAMERON
(OF SEEKAE, SYDNEY)
LOOPHOLE

JUNE 17 2014
BODDINSTAßE 60
21:00

Dan Bodan
Touchy Mob
TEAMS
Phèdre (DJ)
Vero Manchego (DJ)

Dan Bodan
DFA, BERLIN

TOUCHY MOB
BERLIN

teams
LOS ANGELES

11.07.14

DJs
Phèdre (Toronto)
& Vero Manchego (Berlin)

CHESTERS
GLOGAUERSTR.2   23:55

SHAMELESS
/LIMITLESS

UN
Sydney Valette
Bad Orphan (DJ)

It's Tuesday night and
UN
and
Sydney Valette
are making their Berlin debuts and cover charge is real fair and jeez you
remember what happened last time one of these nights came together like
this? I do. Boy, do I ever.

The icing on the cake, as it were, is that Bad Orphan (aka Ryan from
Austra) is going DJ before, between and after the live stuff, so come
early, stay late, tip your bartender etc.

Frances Enyedy

29/07/14
SHAMELESS/
LIMITLESS
PRESENTS
UN
(MONTREAL)
SYDNEY
VALETTE
(PARIS)
DJ Bad Orphan
{AUSTRA}
LOOPHOLE
BODDINSTRAßE 60
21:00

Evy Jane
M.E.S.H.
Why, Alex, Why (DJ)
Better Person (DJ)

SHAMELESS/LIMITLES
BITE CLUB
TORSTRASSEN FESTIVAL

30/08/14

LIVE:

EVY JANE
(NINJA TUNE, VANCOUVER)

M.E.S.H
(PAN, BERLIN)

DJs:

WHY,ALEX,WHY
BETTER PERSON

PLATOON KUNSTHALLE
Schönhauser Allee 9
14:00-22:00

Torn Hawk
Jahiliyya Fields
Privacy (DJ)

Come keep fit, have fun and check out Torn Hawk playing new music from
his upcoming Mexican Summer debut LP "Let's Cry and Do Pushups at the Same
Time". Back catalogue classics and video mulching too because come on,
this is Torn Hawk we're talking here.

Berlin-based weirdo ripper and L.I.E.S recording artist Jahiliyya Fields
will play support.

Natalia Portnoy

NATALIA PORTNOY
Designer

When I moved to Berlin I found myself feeling stranded
and searching for places, friends that I could call my
own. I was looking for music events that had an emotional
impact and a poetic atmosphere, something other than huge
techno raves which I had grown tired of.

I initially connected with Shameless/Limitless online,
and S/L events — usually held in small, cosy and intimate
venues — quickly became my favourite thing about Berlin.

Eventually Kevin from S/L wrote me and asked if I would be
interested in making a flyer for an event. I felt insecure
about my illustration practice, so the invitation was
validating, and motivated me to continue designing.

This invitation started a years-long collaboration
throughout which I've contributed numerous poster
designs and could always count on constructive feedback,
a welcoming attitude and genuine interest in my opinion.
I've experimented with and changed my style over the
years, and have made designs for Alex Cameron (his
show with Pictorial Candi at ACUD being my favourite
contribution), Phèdre (a band who I've stayed in touch
with) and many more.

Even though my main motivation for engaging with S/L
wasn't strictly social, I've met so many absolutely lovely
and talented people through those events and experienced
so much beautiful music — I'm glad we connected all those
years ago.

Heatsick
Mo Probs (DJ)
Renaissance Man (DJ)
Gavin Russom (DJ)
Bill Kouligas (DJ)

27 09 14

SHAMELESS/LIMITLESS

PRESENTS

HEATSICK's
BIRTHDAY PARTY

HEATSICK
(PAN / Berlin / Live)

RENAISSANCE MAN
(Black Ocean)

MO PROBS

GAVIN RUSSOM

+

Special Secret Guests

CHESTERS   Glogauer Straße 2   23:00

Sean Nicholas Savage
Normal Echo
Anton Teichmann (DJ)

Your boyfriend and mine, Sean Nicholas Savage, is back.

Well, I guess he never really left as he's always in our hearts and minds, but I mean he's back in the physical IRL sense, in a singing-those-songs, poeting-those-poems and dancing-those-dances kind of way.

Dream team backing band too, though you'll have to come along to find out what's up there.

No presales / door only.

Sonya Mandus

SHAMELESS/LIMITLESS
PRESENTS

SEAN NICHOLAS SAVAGE
(ARBUTUS, MONTREAL)

NORMAL ECHO
(BERLIN)

Urban Spree Revealer Str 99   20:00   15.10.2014

Alex Cameron
Hush Hush

Red Hot.
Gets thrown around more than it should.
But let me tell you
if you want to see Red Hot — I mean the gold standard, the cream of the
crop, the beaut in the saddle, one to watch for Red Hot — this is your
night.
2 headlining sets
1
from
Alex Cameron — yeah, that Alex Cameron, the one who touched down on our
shores when the sun was out and made a mark something unforgettable,
and
1
from Hush Hush, the locally sourced R&B hitmaker, visionary and performer
extraordinaire.

This one will be priced to your liking and held at Neu West Berlin.

Genevieve Kulesza

SHAMELESS/LIMITLESS
presents an evening with

ALEX
CAMERON
(of Seekae, Sydney)

& Hush
Hush

(Berlin)

28.10.14
Neu West Berlin
Köpenicker Str. 55
21:00

Molly Nilsson
Facit
rRoxymore (DJ)
Dubais (DJ)
S/L (DJ)

Dark Skies Association and Shameless/Limitless proudly present …

SEX

A concert and party in celebration of the release of Molly Nilsson's
first-ever 7″. This little gem comes with two new songs (singles can be
couples too, you know): a duo simply called SEX. Physical copies of the
record will be available for purchase on the night.

Following a DJ set from Dubais and live sets from Molly and Facit,
(who has been flown down from Göteborg especially for the show), there
will be an after party with DJ sets from rRoxymore, Molly Nilsson and
Shameless/Limitless.

All this will take place, fittingly, at the den of inequity that is
Chesters (aka KitKatClub's original location).

Tickets available at the door. Reduced cover charge for the after party.
Please come early to ensure entry, as the venue has limited capacity.

Veronica Manchego

SEX

13/11/14
CHESTERS

DARK SKIES ASSOCIATION

SHAMELESS
/LIMITLESS

White Lung
Dysnea Boys
S/L (DJ)

WHITE LUNG (DOMINO, VANCOUVER)

+ DYSNEA BOYS

15/11/14   WESTGERMANY
SKALITZER STR. 133   21:00

POWERLINE AGENCY & SHAMELESS /LIMITLESS

2014 11 21   SAMEHEADS
                    MAC DEMARCO AFTER PARTY

                    Pierce McGarry (DJ)
                    Joe McMurray (DJ)
                    Andy White (DJ)
                    Juan Wauters (DJ)
                    Thieves Like Us (DJ)
                    Jason Harvey (DJ)

Mac DeMarco is playing a sold-out show in Berlin on a Friday night and
you thought we wouldn't get some kind of after party together? GTFOH, no
chance, of course we got ourselves an after party together and it's a hot
one too — DJ sets from Juan Wauters (Captured Tracks), Thieves Like Us
(also Captured Tracks), ascendant local Jayyce (I see you Jason Harvey)
and also get this how sweet is this, Pierce, Joe and Andy from Mac's band
are going to MC / DJ / keep festivities spirited and greasy.

€3/5 w/without ticket for the show.

Jason Harvey

100% OFFICIAL
MAC DEMARCO
AFTER PARTY
BERLIN 2K14 *Featuring*

What's not to like?

MARK DEMARCO©

SAMEHEADS
RICHARDSTR 10
3/5 €
W/WITHOUT
TICKET
22.30

DJ DANCE BASS

PIERCE MCGARRY FROM tOilet.com!

DJ DUMPSTER

100% HARRY LEGAL
MAC DEMARCO RAVE BAR

WITH
ADDITIONAL
DJING BY

JUAN WAUTERS
(CAPTURED TRACKS)

DJ JASON HARVEY
EUROPE'S
MOST aLtErNaTiVe
MUSIC DJ

NOVEMBER 21ST
SO CLOSE 2 MY
BIRTHDAY

THIEVES LIKE US
(CAPTURED TRACKS)

MUSIC

SHAMELESS /LIMITLESS
PUSCHEN

Golden Donna
SFTSTPS
N1L
Jayyce
Olle Holmberg (DJ)

You are cordially invited to take a Friday night road trip up north for
S/L's first dalliance with ACUD. 4 live acts, 1 stellar DJ and cheap cover
charge — kind of makes you want to start planning your journey already,
doesn't it?

Golden Donna (100% Silk, Madison)

N1L (Riga)
It's all very hush-hush for now, but it is a safe Gamble that big things
are coming soon for N1L.

SFTSTPS (Berlin)
First show back in Berlin from this true-blue weirdo ripper. Always a treat.

Jayyce (Berlin)
Europe's most alternative music DJ (hi Jason Harvey) will be stepping out
and showcasing his own stuff. If Jayyce produces Europe's most alternative
music remains to be seen.

Olle Holmberg (aka Moon Wheel) will be DJing before, between and after
the live stuff like only he knows how.

Guy Torsher

TOPS
Feelings

NOVEMBER 30TH 2014

PUSCHEN & SHAMELESS LIMITLESS

present

SUNDAY FUNDAY

PART 3

AN AFTERNOON DELIGHT

with

TOPS (ARBUTUS, MONTREAL)

---

and **FEELINGS** (BERLIN)

+ DJS / NAIL ART / MASSAGES / ZINES / TASTY TREATS AND MORE!

---

at MONARCH

SKALITZER STR 134

BERLIN

DOORS: 4PM

SHOW: 5PM

Naomi Punk
Plattenbau

2015 02 05   CHESTERS

Magic Island
Jack Chosef
Lief Hall
Better Person
DJ Deepmoods
Karl Monica (DJ)
Normal Echo (DJ)

Moritz Freudenberg

Shameless Limitless with Mansions and Millions presents:

Magic Island - Wasted Dawn EP Release Party

with guests:

Jack Chosef (Mansions and Millions)
Lief Hall (Berlin)
Better Person (Live Premiere)

After Party with:

DJ Deepmoods
Karl Monica

05/02/15 21:00

Chesters

SHAMELESS LIMITLESS

Mansions & Millions

EXBERLINER

ADAM BYCZKOWSKI
Better Person

Back in 2015, Shameless/Limitless
hosted my first-ever solo show
as Better Person at Chesters
Club, a now forgotten venue with
a shady past.

I was so scared of performing
alone that (as my manager Anton
remembers it) I asked Kevin if
I could quickly play before the
doors were even open to the public.

I can't remember the show at all —
I was very drunk when I walked on
stage, right after puking up the
delish Azzam catering.

Even though this doesn't sound
like much fun, it truly was. I
miss those times.

Pender Street Steppers (DJ)
Omer (DJ)
Physical Therapy (DJ)
Criese (DJ)

Mmmmmm mmm. Nice As. Like a kit kat on your coffee break. Like a gatorade after a 5k fun run. Like a cheeky marlboro when your better half steps out for a mani-pedi. Like a mani-pedi — the nice ones with the hand massages and maybe the fish nibblers too. Like Pender Street Steppers (Mood Hut, Vancouver) laying down musical tracks that make you feel all right, all through the night. Like taking the hit to make the play and then putting in the work to get back on your feet and then getting back on your feet and going to the club and enjoying the sounds that Physical Therapy (Allergy Season, Berlin) is choosing to put out over the loudspeakers. Like stopping in at your favourite backfactory on your way home from work to grab your favourite backtreat, only to be treated to a wink and a smile from your favourite backfactory counter girl. Like putting your feet up because the long weekend is here and you're looking forward to being treated to one of Omer's always stunning deejay sets. Like after having had your feet up in advance of and then actually being at the club for Omer's (Cocktail d'Amore, Berlin) deejay set. Like thinking that it would be a fun idea to have a party and then finding out that one of the gold bearers of Berlin nightlife — I'm talking Criese here, people — has confirmed that he's on board. It'll be like that. What a world.

Apostille
Happy Meals
Molly Nilsson (DJ)
Better Person (DJ)
Better Person's Better Person (DJ)

I'm no scientist.

My money doesn't come from running the numbers
or producing the potions or knowing the difference between your UVs and
your SPFs and your USBs.

Nonetheless, I've been doing some thinking, been doing some looking when
I ought to look and some attention-paying when attention needs to be paid.

It took a minute, but I got there. I got here. I'm ready to submit an
equation to the texts or the wikis or wherever it is that the sciencers
put their knowings:

S/L x SameHeads = Assured Satisfaction. AS. AS HYFR. Every time.
Full stop.

To wit, i.e. pudding with the proof, i.e. here's where it gets good:

04/04/15
Shameless/Limitless Presents …
Apostille (Night School, London)
Happy Meals (Night School, Glasgow)
+ DJs
Molly Nilsson
Better Person
Better Person's Better Person
Sameheads Berlin

23:00 — End

Gudrun Jonsdottir

SHAMELESS
/LIMITLESS Presents...
APOSTILLE
(Night School Records, London)
HAPPY MEALS
(Night School Records, Glasgow)
+DJs
MOLLY NILSSON
(Dark Skies Association)
BETTER PERSON
(Mansions & Millions)
BETTER PERSON'S
BETTER PERSON
04/04/15
Sameheads
23:00

Antoine93
COUNTRY
Ben Jackson (DJ)

Shameless/Limitless presents a MTL dream team double-double with
headlining sets from all in all the time go-getter Antoine93 + the Berlin
debut of sleaze-wave savants and culinary MVPs COUNTRY.

Oh also for a little icing on the cake by way of Ben Jackson on the MP3s
before between and after the live stuff. Put it in the book — we've got
a Thursday shaker on our hands.

Priced right, so that you'll have some argent left over for the dep and
after-hours poutine.

Antoine Lahaie

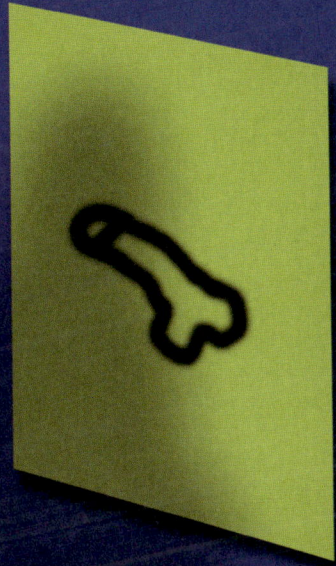

SHAMELESS
/ LIMITLESS

presents

an evening with

ANTOINE93
(Montreal, Mansions & Millions)

COUNTRY
(Montreal)

09.04.2015
LOOPHOLE
20:30

2015 04 24   **LOOPHOLE**

> **Dubais**
> **Goldweiner**
> **Skiing (Cancelled)**
> **Molly Nilsson (DJ)**
> **S/L (DJ)**

If you're here
looking for me to tell you
that
Dubais
is putting out a 7″
and is playing a show to celebrate that
and has invited Goldweiner to also play live
and
Molly Nilsson and S/L to DJ
well
I got news:
you're in the right spot.

That being the case,
Dubais is putting out a 7″
and is playing a show to celebrate
and has invited Goldweiner to play live
and
Molly Nilsson and S/L to DJ.

Far out, right arm, real cool – just 3 of the emotions I feel telling you
about this. Lots more where those came from.

/*/*/*/*You were going to hear it soon enough so you might as well hear it
here: Skiing had to cancel. Tis a shame, as plans were afoot to coronate
them prom royalty.****\

Holly Mia

DUBAIS
ep release show

Skiing

Molly Nilsson (DJ)

Goldweiner

LOOPHOLE
24.04.15
22.00

SHAMELESS
/LIMITLESS

Father Murphy
Lief Hall

EINE WELT AUS HACK & SHAMELESS/LIMITLESS:

FATHER MURPHY

HALL

WESTGERMANY
05.05.2015
BERLIN

2015 05 26   WESTGERMANY

Wand
Plattenbau (DJ)

L. Zylberberg

TOPS
Better Person

Doomsquad
Helen Fry
Touchy Mob (DJ)

How rad is this? New Bella Union signees, old Shameless/Limitless
favourites and recent Fucked Up tourmates DOOMSQUAD are back in Berlin for
their third time in as many years. Support comes in the form of a rare
performance from Helen Fry.

Bonus: the one and only Touchy Mob is going to MP3 before, between,
and a little after the live stuff.

Natalia Portnoy

DOOMSQUAD
(Bella Union,Toronto)

HELEN FRY
(BERLIN)

SHAMELESS/LIMITLESS
02/06/2015
20:30
Loophole

Jaakko Eino Kalevi
Long-Sam
Molly Nilsson (DJ)
Chikiss (DJ)

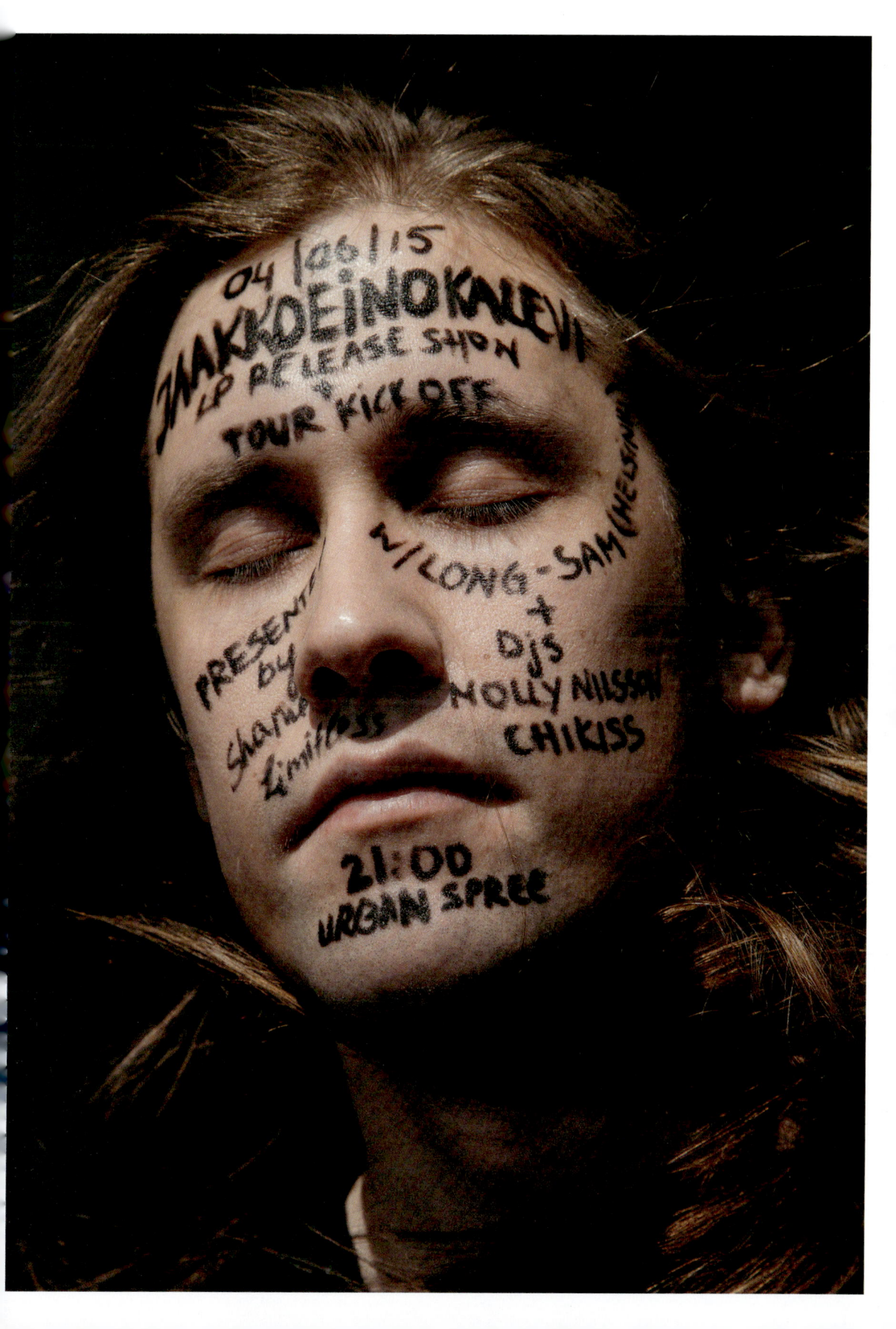

S/L & Friends

Every second Wednesday from 10 to end!
Free shot of mexicaner w/ purchase of beer!

SHAMELESS LIMITLESS

Das Gift

X

EVERY SECOND WEDNESDAY

22:00 UNTIL THE END

UPCOMING DATES:

24.06: WITH PUSCHEN DJS

08.07: BLUE DRINKS — DADDISON EXHIBITION SPECIAL!

22.07 **05.08** **19.08**

FREE MEXICANER WITH EVERY BEER

DAS GIFT. DONAUSTRASSE 119. 12043 BERLIN. DASGIFT.TUMBLR.COM

DAVID ADDISON
Artist
Designer

Remember when Karl Lagerfeld came to that Sameheads party with his miniature Dalmatian puppy that was wearing tiny golden Reebok Classics?

Or when the smoke machine jammed at Loophole on a Dienstag and everyone was kissing everyone then a Bruce Springsteen greatest hits playlist played on repeat for 6 hours and it seemed like no-one noticed?

That one night during fashion week with the Super Moon at (I think) Monarch with the giant inflatable thing and them big blue Garys and the oversized pupils all the way to Schönefeld. Très Espresso!

The pre-dinner for whoever's birthday of endless bouillabaisse served in the Versace dinner sets with that funny green herbal drink I like that they sell at every Spätkauf?

When the basement at Naherholung Sternchen was converted into a full-functioning ice rink and a Lidl bag full of crumpled 5 euro notes was the prize for a dancing-on-ice-off?

The inappropriate marriage proposal on the dancefloor at WestGermany? I was livid.

When we got snowed in for 5 hours in the back room of Internet Explorer by "The Great Storm"™ and all the staff had gone home and 9 people had to keep warm with only 2 bottles of Highland Park 18-year-old malt while playing snake on Eric's Nokia?

The secret-location-out-of-town party at that place with the marble tiles and mother of pearl door knobs and neon exit signs everywhere and complimentary Shameless/Limitless-branded cashmere robes for all ticket holders? And the next day we went skinny-dipping in the Med and ate fried sea urchin for lunch?

Sunday after-party thing where it was free entry if you could prove you had set an out-of-office auto-responder to your primary email otherwise €20 in and absolutely no use of the cloak room under any circumstances?

The 2C-B magic arm touch night at Das Gift where everyone was sharking around the non-existent dance floor then that Spanish pop star fell over in the toilet and broke one of the football goal-shaped urinals and someone fired a rocket right at the window so we locked the door

2015 07 26   URBAN SPREE

          Foxtrott
          Antoine93
          Why, Alex, Why (DJ)

Pascale Mercier

FOXTROTT
(ONE LITTLE INDIAN. MONTREAL)

ANTOINE93
(MANSIONS & MILLIONS. BERLIN)

WHY ALEX. WHY (DJ)

July 26th . Urban Spree . 9pm

SHAMELESS LIMITLESS

POWERLINE AGENCY

Melting Hearts
Slow Steve
Islaja (DJ)

Helen Fry
BifiBoy
Karolini (DJ)

In collaboration with c.project
Shameless/Limitless presents
a show
up high
in the sky
with
Helen Fry
and BifiBoy
on the 8th floor of
Greenhouse.

Karolini will be on MP3s before, between and a little after the live stuff.

Saturday night though this may be, this will be an early affair.
That is to say, if you're late, we won't wait.

Jeongkyoung Woo

c. project

**Live On The 8th Floor of
Greenhouse Berlin _ Plateau Gallery
Gottlieb-Dunkel-Str. 43/44
20:00   29. Aug. 2015**

**Helen Fry (Berlin)
BiFi Boy (Berlin)**

Shameless/Limitless

Russo
Divine Diamond
Torn Hawk (DJ)

My hope
is that
you like these Loophole things
as much as I do.
2 shows in a week might seem indulgent
but what
you think I'm not going to put on a lineup like this when it comes
a-knockin'?

What we have here is we have the Berlin debut of an NYC-based, Valcrond
Video-signed, VHS videomulch artist and versatile producer who goes
by Russo.

Mexican Summer-signed and long-established scene fixture Torn Hawk will
be stepping out on the MP3s, playing all manner of things that make a mind
like his tick.

Divine Diamond consist of Privacy and Alobhe.
This is their first … and potentially last show.

Priced right, placed right, what more do you need?

Jorge H. Loureiro

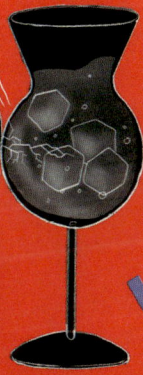

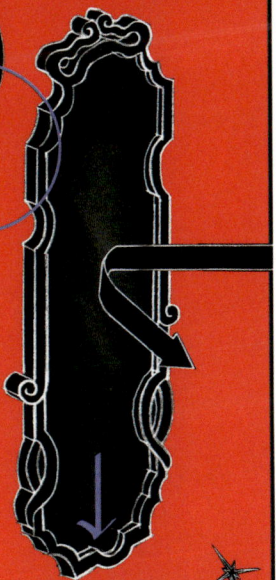

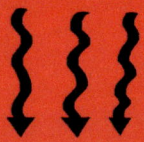

Palmbomen II
Bahamian Moor (DJ)
Omer (DJ)
W/ndows (DJ)

Strikes me plain as day that we've got ourselves a real good thing here.
Real good party. One worth coming out for. One worth gearing up for.
One worth counting down the days to. One worth saving yr coins up for.
One worth savourin' through and through, from start to finish.

Let me tell you what a party like this looks like: a live set from the
Beats In Space-signed, Los Angeles-based Palmbomen II, + also deejay sets
from perpetual up-and-comer / established scene fixture Omer (Cocktail
d'Amore), Dance Café-releasing out-of-towners (and NTS radio stars)
Bahamian Moor, and, the icing on the cake, old S/L friend and fixer,
W/ndows (FKA Night Angles).

Rest assured, the price point has been set with your interests in mind.
All you gotta do is show up — we've got the rest taken care of.

Tim Eve

SHAMELESS/LIMITLESS PRESENTS...

PALMBOMEN II
(BEATS IN SPACE, LOS ANGELES)

+DJS

OMER
(COCKTAIL D'AMORE, BERLIN)

BAHAMIAN MOOR
(DANCE CAFE, LONDON)

WINDOWS
(BERLIN)

SAMEHEADS

5/9/15

23:00

Juan Wauters
Jason Harvey
King Khan (DJ)

Following previous editions which featured Skiing, TOPS, Dent May and Mac
DeMarco, Puschen and Shameless/Limitless have teamed up again to bring you
another Sunday Funday Afternoon Delight.

This sesh includes NYC's resident heartthrob weirdo (and rising Captured
Tracks recording artist) Juan Wauters, a DJ set from King Khan (of King
Khan And The Shrines) and a performative multimedia extravaganza from
local favourite Jason Harvey.

BUT THAT'S NOT ALL:

Super rad illustrators Aisha Franz and Lasse Wandschneider will be selling
zines, Massage with Morrissey will be doling out massages, Adrienne
Kammerer will be doing stick-and-poke tattoos and there will also be tasty
treats for eatin' for sale too.

What I can tell you with certainty is that this is an afternoon event.
Doors at 16:00, live stuff starts around 17:00.

Lewis Lloyd

puschen & shameless/limitless present

SUNDAYFUNDAY

an afternoon delight with:

juan wauters
(Captured Tracks, NYC)

king khan (DJ)

a digital multimedia presentation
by
jason harvey

omg it is all so beautiful

+ Pizza / Zines/ Massages & Maybe More? 😛

13.09.15 Monarch, Skalitzerstr. 134 Doors 16:00

Molly Nilsson
Apostille
Alex Cameron
Planningtorock (DJ)
S/L (DJ)

Dark Skies Association and Shameless/Limitless proudly present Molly
Nilsson, live in concert in celebration of the impending release of her
new LP, Zenith.

Special guests Apostille (Live), Alex Cameron (Live) & Planningtorock (DJ).

Zenith

15/09/15

2015 09 18   URBAN SPREE
                    MAC DEMARCO AFTER PARTY

                    Walter TV
                    Andy Boay
                    Joe McMurray (DJ)
                    Molly Nilsson (DJ)
                    Barry Burns (DJ)
                    Jason Harvey (DJ)
                    No Drama (DJ)
                    RoommateZ (DJ)
                    Karolini (DJ)

Another one?
Yes, let's. 2 floors with a whole lot of action to choose from, including
…

Live:
Walter TV (feat Joe and Pierce of Mac's band — Berlin debut!)
Andy Boay (solo project from Andy, who plays in Mac's band +
TONSTARTSSBANDHT)

MP3s:
Joe McMurray (aka DJ Dumpster aka on the drums)
Molly Nilsson
Barry Burns (of Mogwai)
Jason Harvey
DJ No Drama (aka Adrienne Kammerer)
RoomateZ (aka Rhianne McNally and Philip Diep of Mona Lisa Disco)
Karoloni

Reduced entry for Mac DeMarco ticket holders.

Jason Harvey

LOOPHOLE

Oscar Key Sung
Alex Cameron (DJ)

Kevin Halpin

S *melbourne* ung

A lex

K ey

C *sydney*

O scar

ameron (DJ)

06/10/15
loophole
21:00

SHAMELESS
/LIMITLESS

DANIELLE RAHAL
Designer
Lolsnake
Weeeirdos

When I arrived in Berlin in 2014, I went to a myriad
of events around the city, in search of a grasp
on the different communities that exist under the
vast umbrella that is the local music scene.

It wasn't long until I stumbled upon Shameless/
Limitless, perfectly hidden in plain sight. With
beautiful, uniquely designed posters for each
event, and interesting and relevant lineups which
always featured a combination of artists I wanted
to see, or had never heard of, S/L felt real, raw
and had a sense of humour too. I didn't miss a
single event for a few years.

It also didn't take long to notice the rich community
of artists and attendees that are all connected
through Shameless/Limitless — a discovery which
was, and still is inspiring to me. I was pretty
happy to be asked to make a show poster a few years
ago. At some point after that, Kevin pushed me into
starting my own event series (Weeeirdos). He was
encouraging, which helped, as I was not even sure
I could organize my own events — I had always just
been an avid event attendee.

The existence of Shameless/Limitless has enriched
the city so much and also offered space for people
like me to run with new ideas, and to create new
platforms with similar goals, which is no doubt an
asset to the Berlin scene.

2015 10 09   CHESTERS
                    1080P LABEL NIGHT

                    Project Pablo (DJ)
                    Dan Bodan (DJ)
                    Max McFerren (DJ)
                    Scientific Dreamz of U (DJ)

Shameless/Limitless is hopeful that this gentle digital nudge will
lead you to attend this, the 1080p label night, with DJ sets from
roster highlights Dan Bodan, Project Pablo, Scientific Dreamz of
U & Max McFerren. Nudge nudge, wink wink.

ツ ツ ツ ツ ツ ツ ツ ツ ツ ツ ツ ツ ツ ツ ツ ツ ツ ツ

Jason Harvey

Moon Wheel
Body Tools
Night Musik (DJ)

Well lookee here,
Tuesday night party sesh at Loophole with:
Moon Wheel (Berlin)
Body Tools — A new collaborative project consisting of Torn Hawk and Xosar
— first show!!
and
Night Musik (DJ).
Good price, great place, swell jams. Right arm, man.

SHAMELESS/ LIMITLESS

PRESENTS

Moon Wheel (Berlin)

Body Tools (Torn Hawk x Xosar -- First Show!)

LOOPHOLE

13/10/2015

Night Musik (DJ, Berlin)

20:30

U.S. Girls
S/L (DJ)

29
10
MONARCH

20
00
SKALITZERSTR.
134

U.

S.

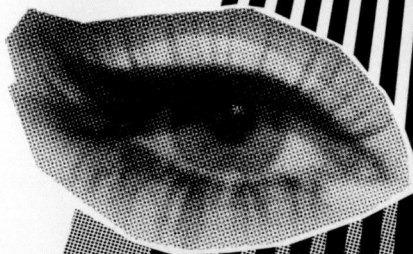
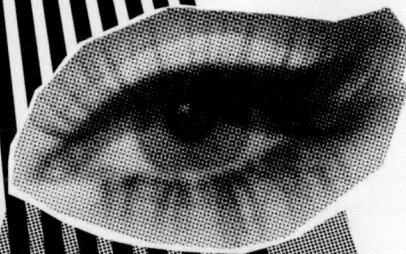

GIRLS

(4AD, TORONTO)

SHAMELESS⚡
LIMITLESS⚡

spex

PUSCHEN

Sean Nicholas Savage
Touchy Mob

06/11/15

Puschen and
Shameless/Limitless
Present...

Senn Nicholas Savage

Arbutus, Montréal

Touchy Mob

Leipzig

Urban Spree
20:00

Kirin J Callinan
Touchy Mob (DJ)
Sean Nicholas Savage (DJ)
Princess Century (DJ)
DENA (DJ)
Karl Monica (DJ)
No Drama (DJ)

Ripperpoodley
it's on:
the after party.
Following Sean Nicholas Savage + Touchy Mob's show
we're gonna have ourselves a time that's real good
with
Kirin J Callinan (live)
+ DJ sets from
Touchy Mob
Sean Nicholas Savage
Princess Century (Austra / Trust)
DENA (!K7)
Karl Monica
&
No Drama.

Reduced entry for show ticket holders.

Moritz Freudenberg

06/11/15

The After Party

Shameless/Limitless Presents ...

Kirin J Callinan
XL, Sydney

Sean Nicholas Savage
sucks
Arbutus, Montréal

Touchy Mob
hot
Leipzig

Princess Century
fo sho
Austral/Trust, Brussels

DENA
OMG
!K7, Berlin

No Drama
No Way!
Berlin

Karl Monica
cute
Berlin

(Urban Spree)

Moss Lime
Tendre Biche
Skiing (DJ)

Magic Island
Pictorial Candi
Mona Lisa Disco (DJ)

Moritz Freudenberg

21/11/15
Shameless/Limitless presents...

Magic Island
(Mansions and ... rlin)

Pictorial Candi
(Warsaw)

Mona Lisa Djs
(Berlin)

at
ACUD, 21:00

Majical Cloudz
Jason Harvey

Never Work & Shameless/Limitless present

MAJI

Majical Cloudz (Canada / Matador)

CAL

Special guest: Jason Harvey (the artist)

CLOU

Wednesday, 25th of November, 8pm

DZ

Acud Club, Berlin

2015 11 30   WESTGERMANY

        Alex Calder
        Weyes Blood
        Sean Nicholas Savage (DJ)

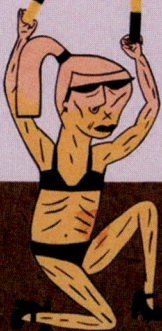

RYAN ROSELL
DJ Darmok
Tennis Bar
The Chop

It is October 15th, 2014. I have just moved to Berlin and am still suffering from unremitting, anxiety-induced diarrhea. I am standing in Urban Spree surrounded by people, many of whom will become my dearest friends. Sean Nicholas Savage is playing. After the show I introduce myself to Kevin. We ride our bikes together to the after party at Das Gift and for the first time we discuss "business".

It is November 21st, 2014. I am on a bad Tinder date at the Mac DeMarco after party in Sameheads. Jason Harvey is DJing. We do not meet, but later he will become my best friend. My Tinder date says she is going to leave. I say "Okay."

It is July 13th, 2018. Kevin and I are discussing "business" in the ground floor-level cafe of the Neukölln Arcaden. We are planning a festival that will eventually be called No Kiddin'. After we agree this is a good idea and our meeting concludes, we realize that we are both going to do grocery shopping downstairs at Kaufland. It's awkward. We bid each other farewell and try to do our shopping without making further eye contact.

It is August 19th, 2019. Kev (I call him "Kev" now) and I are standing behind the sound desk at Internet Explorer watching our co-promoted, sold-out Crack Cloud show. Kev leans over to say something that I do not hear. "What?", I ask. But he does not repeat himself.

Dylan III
Antoine93
Linnea Palmestål (DJ)

Novella
Fake Laugh
Lui Voetton (DJ)

Puschen and Shameless/Limitless present another edition of the always fun,
always day, always Sunday, Sunday Funday. This time with NOVELLA, Fake
Laugh, karaoke with Johanna and Dayna, stick-and-poke tattoos and more.
Reduced entry if yr on a Tinder date.

NOVELLA
SINDERLYN RECORDS, LONDON

FAKE LAUGH
LONDON

KARAOKE
TATTOOS
TASTY TREATS
& MORE

DJ LUI VOETTON
(TENORE BICHE)

SO. 14.02. 16.00
MONARCH
SKALITZERSTR. 134

SUNDAY
FUNDAY

LARSMARIA

SHAMELESS
/LIMITLESS   PUSCHEN   AN AFTERNOON EXTRAVAGANZA

Jaakko Eino Kalevi
Melting Hearts

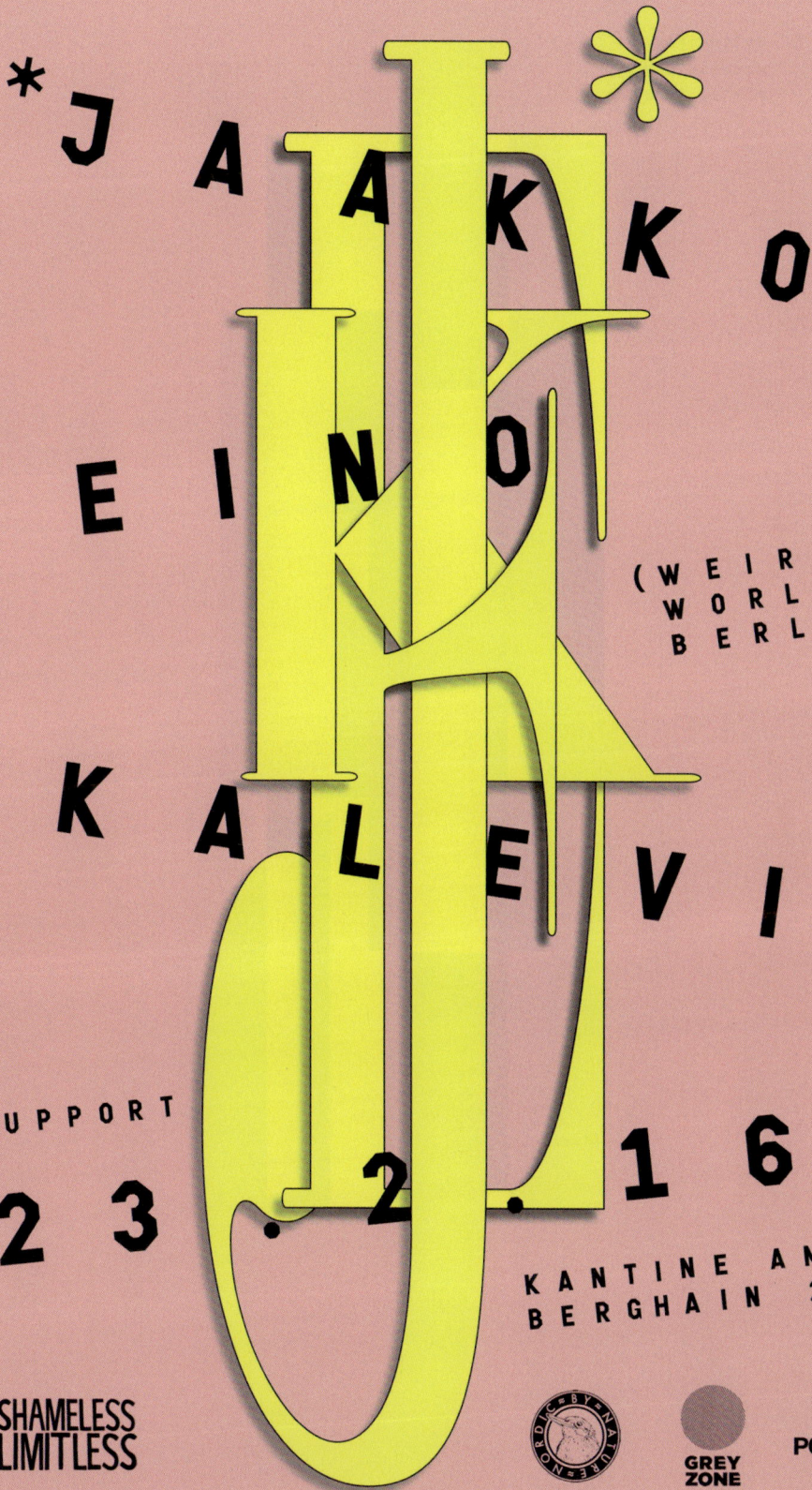

*JAAKKO *

EINO

KALEVI

(WEIRD
WORLD
BERLIN)

+SUPPORT 23.2.16

KANTINE AM
BERGHAIN 20.00

SHAMELESS
LIMITLESS

GREY
ZONE

POWERLINE
AGENCY

2016 02 25   URBAN SPREE

                    Better Person
                    Promise Keeper
                    Philip FM (DJ)

Moritz Freudenberg

Puschen and Shameless / Limitless present

an EP release night with

Better Person

supported by

Promise Keeper

25.02.2016   Urban Spree   9:00pm

Plattenbau
Skiing
Raised on Robbery (DJ)

Shameless/Limitless proudly presents local go-getters Plattenbau for
a final hometown show before they endeavour to win over SXSW and
subsequently the entirety of the USA. While we're at it, we might as well
also celebrate the release of the band's new tape. See what I mean about
being go-getters?

Support comes from the persistently consistent, thoroughly excellent
Skiing.

Raised on Robbery will DJ before, between, and a lil after the live stuff.

Tickets available at the door only.

Alexandra Aquilina

PLATTENBAU
Album Release + US Tour Kick-Off Show

+ Skiing (Berlin)
Raised on Robbery (DJs)

Monarch
06/03/16
20:00

SHAMELESS
LIMITLESS ⚡
PRESENTS

Project Pablo (DJ)
Bluntman Deejay aka House Of Doors (DJ)
Bahamian Moor (DJ)
W/ndows (DJ)

~ Makin' a real big cannonball-sized splash at Sameheads with:

Project Pablo (1080p, Montréal)
Bluntman Deejay aka House Of Doors (Mood Hut, Vancouver)
Bahamian Moor (NTS Radio, London)
W/ndows (Berlin)

And, it's gotta be said: It feels good, man. ~

Brought to you with a little help from my friends at no fear of pop.

Mark Stroemich

SHAMELESS LIMITLESS Presents:

GOLDENER PREIS 2015 · WWW.DLG.ORG

SAMEHEADS BEST UNDERGROUND NIGHT CLUB IN BERLIN

SameHeads 23:00
March 11, 2016

Project Pablo (1080p, Montréal)
House Of Doors ~ aka Bluntman Deejay ~ (Mood Hut, Vancouver)
Bahamian Moor (NTS Radio, London)
Windows (Berlin)

Palmbomen II
Via App
Seekae (DJ)
Heatsick (DJ)
Broshuda (DJ)

Well if you really wanna know, yeah, I suppose it will be some kind of
dance performance.

S/L's 1st time at St. Georg. Going all in with:

Palmbomen II (Beats in Space / 1080p, LA)
Seekae (DJ — Future Classic, Sydney)
Via App (1080p, NYC)
Heatsick (DJ — PAN, Berlin)
Broshuda (DJ — Sonic Router, Berlin)

A legitimately good time is to be had, partic so if you are predisposed to
be into this kinda thing. That helps, but isn't required. First timers and
curious types are also welcome. You're all welcome. Bring money.

Broshuda

SHAMELESSLIMITLESS
PRESENTS

PALMBOMEN II
BEATS IN SPACE/ LA

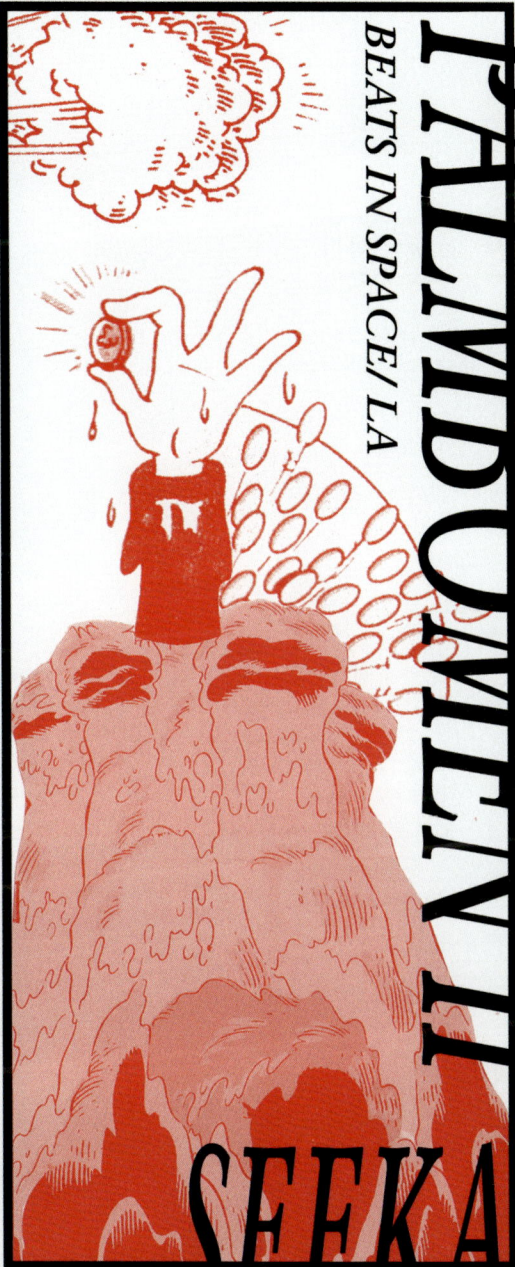

SEEKAE
DJ - FUTURE CLASSIC/ SYD

HEATSICK
DJ - PAN/BLN

VIA APP
1080/NYC

DESIGN - BROSHUDA

01/04/16
23:00
ST. GEORG

Pictorial Candi
Exit Someone
Karolini (DJ)
Robert Bęza (VJ)

Shameless/Limitless warmly welcomes Warsaw scene queen (and recent
Mansions & Millions signee) Pictorial Candi, live in concert in
celebration and observance of the release of her new music video.

Exit Someone will be playing support. This will be their first show.
They include members of Vesuvio Solo, and, based on what I've heard,
they sound just right. Perfect for a thing like this.

Much-loved NK fixture Karolini will be DJing before // between // after.

SHAMELESS/LIMITLESS presents

Pictorial Candi

Mansions & Millions, Warsaw

support: *Exit Someone*

featuring members of Vesuvio solo

DJ Karolini
VJ Robert Bęza
Loophole
07.04.2016

Sean Nicholas Savage

Shameless/Limitless proudly presents

an intimate evening with

Sean Nicholas Savage.

Playing songs new, old and always excellent.

Solo.
Vulnerable.
Present.
Perfect.
Mostly perfect.
Trying to be perfect.
Aren't we all?
Limited capacity — come early.

12/05/16
Shameless/Limitless
Presents...
An Evening With
Sean Nicholas
Savage (Arbutus,
Berlin)
Loophole
21:00

> **Klein**
> **Lamin Fofana (DJ)**
> **Scientific Dreamz of U (DJ)**
> **Covco (DJ)**
> **Sarah Miles (DJ)**
> **Anastasia Filipovna (DJ)**

Yeah that's right,
you guessed it.
Right on the money.
Your intuition is sharp.
Your ability to deduce is on point.
Your gut feeling yields accurate results:
We're having a party and everyone's invited.

It'll be like this:
Klein (Live, London)
Lamin Fofana (SCI-FI & FANTASY, NYC)
Scientific Dreamz of U (1080p, London)
Covco (NTS Radio, London)
BCR DJs

~Brought to you with a lil help from our friends at no fear of pop.~

KLEIN
LIVE — LONDON
LAMIN FOFANA
SCI-FI & FANTASY
SCIENTIFIC DREAMZ OF U
1080P COLLECTION
COVCONTS
ANASTASIA FILIPOVNA
SARAH MILES
OHM BERLIN MAY 13
DOORS 23:30
KÖPENICKER 70

ANASTAZJA MOSER
Anastasia Filipovna
Berlin Community Radio Co-founder and Director
Linda Lee

It felt important to weave Shameless/Limitless into the mesh of Berlin Community Radio as, in a city dominated by electronic music, S/L stood out by constantly putting in work, putting on shows, booking small and bigger bands and cultivating a community of Berlin-based musicians. A regular monthly show followed, as did wonderful S/L show posters plastered around BCR studios.

We put on a party together at OHM, bringing Klein for her debut Berlin show, alongside fellow Londoner Covco, recent Sierra Leonean via NYC transplant Lamin Fofana and BCR residents. The party was a success and I remember long after Klein reminiscing on how "Berlin is the opposite to London, you guys love to book someone completely unknown and everyone is so into it, packing a club."

I've always been excited to play S/L parties, which I love for their eclectic lineups and DIY vibe. My favourite shows were the 9 Years S/L anniversary and the No Kiddin' festival, both of which took place at Internet Explorer, a classic Neukölln industrial warehouse venue. I played my usual shit show of mixing Santana into DJ Khaled followed by a happy eurotrance remix, all to a floor of enthusiastic partygoers.

Homeshake
WEDDING
Fenster (DJ)

Puschen and Shameless/Limitless, together yet again, savouring comped
beers and flexing their organizational and promotional muscle all in
the name of bringing you, the beloved punter, the Berlin debut of
rad music-making outfit Homeshake. Support comes courtesy of Berlin /
Manchester-based young guns WEDDING. Fenster will see to MP3s before /
between / a lil after the live stuff.

The Seth Bogart Show
Miserable Lesbians

the seth bogart show

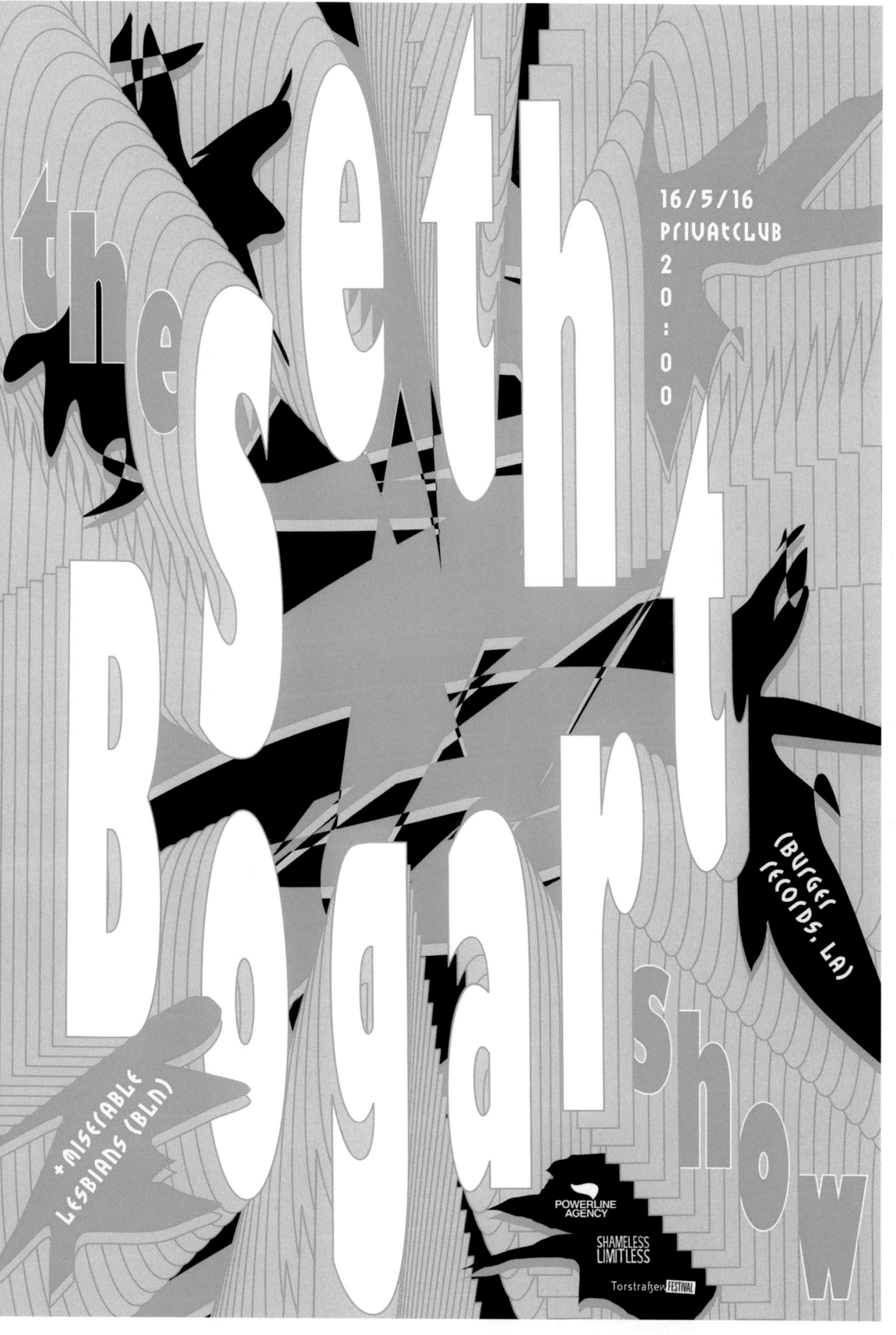

16/5/16
privatCLUB
20:00

(Burger
records, LA)

+miserable
Lesbians (BLN)

POWERLINE
AGENCY

SHAMELESS
LIMITLESS

Torstraßen FESTIVAL

Geneva Jacuzzi
Bobbypin
Norman Palm (DJ)

28/05/16

SHAMELESS/LIMITLESS

+

NO FEAR OF POP

PRESENT

GENEVA JACUZZI
LOS ANGELES

BOBBY PIN
BERLIN

WESTGERMANY   21:00

Torn Hawk
CFCF
Blue Hawaii (DJ)
Omer (DJ)

LIVE TORN
HAWK

MEXICAN SUMMER

CFCF

1080P

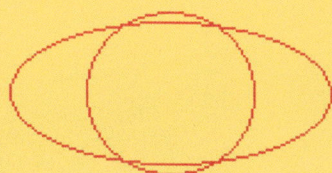

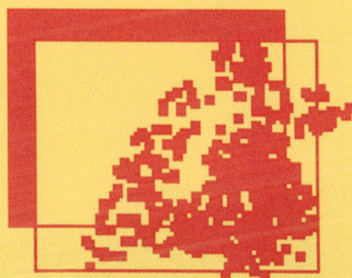

DJ
BLUE
HAWAII

ARBUTUS

OMER

COCKTAIL
D'AMORE

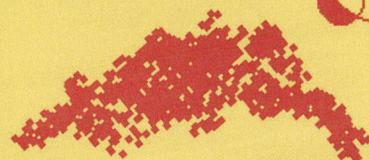

BROSHUDA SEMJ

STGEORG NO DOGS 23:55 17062016

LOOPHOLE

Ramzi
Regular Fantasy

regularfantasy

RAMZi

june 23 ✳ LOOPHOLE
BERLIN

Sad Eyes
Aporia
Educated Body (DJ)

infinite bisous
Jason Harvey
Alex Cameron (DJ)
Roy Molloy (DJ)

How's this for a tasty morsel?

infinite bisous (he of occasional Mac DeMarco and Connan Mockasin band membership, and of supreme songwriting craftsmanship) is comin' to town, and he's playin' at Loophole.

Jason Harvey will descend from his perch and don his 3d toilet crown for a support performance consisting of some manner of spoken word majesty.

Alex Cameron, aka the hardest-working guy online aka world-class support act aka S/L's close personal confidante and advisor will be on MP3s before, between and after. I'm also schilling out an appearance fee for Roy Molloy, in case that gets your wallet open.

~V peng jams comin' your way~

~previously announced Sad Eyes had to pull chute on account of gettin' his ins and outs confused~

Rory McCarthy

shameless/limitless presents

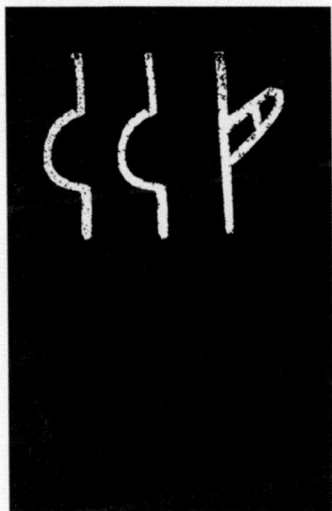

infinite bisous
(tasty morsels, paris)

jason harvey
(3d toilet, berlin)

alex cameron w/ roy molloy
(DJ, secretly canadian, sydney)

loophole berlin
28/07/16
21:00

Ara Koufax (DJ)
Rezzie Avissar (DJ)
No_drama (DJ)
Off-Kultur DJs

In anticipation of Off-Kultur, Shameless/Limitless and (˘ ³˘) are putting
on a celebratory function at Loophole Berlin. Please come early and stay
late, all the while enjoying the propulsive party selections of booked DJs

Ara Koufax (Cutters Records, Melbourne)
Rezzie Avissar (1080p / Weird Magic, NYC)
No_drama (Berlin)
Off-Kultur DJs

Entry is cheap as Kland Western Geschmack BBQ chips well not quite but
relatively speaking you get the idea also feel free to bring a lil snack
if that's gonna help you get right.

Baly Gaudin

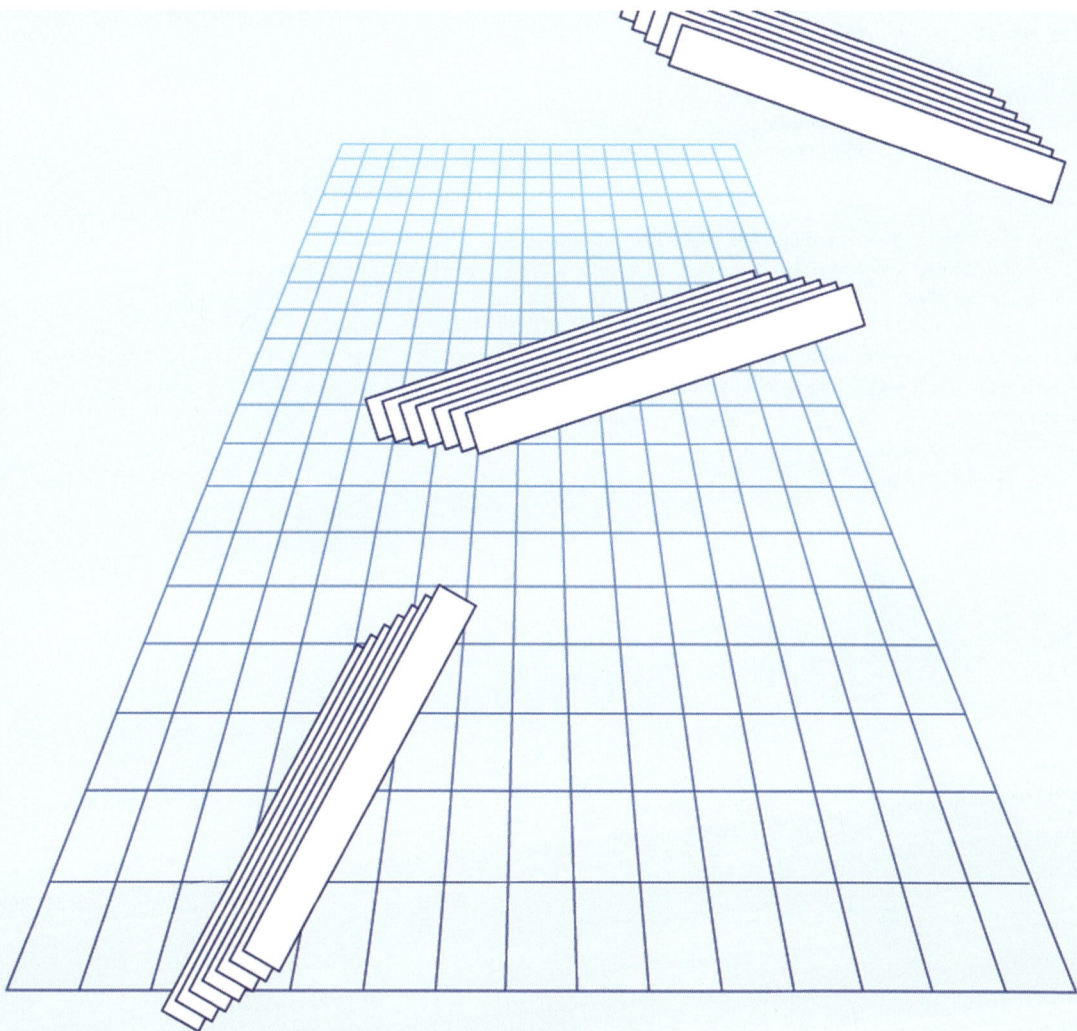

Ara Koufax CUTTERS RECORDS MELBOURNE

Rezzie Avissar 1080P/WEIRD MAGIC NYC

No_drama BERLIN

Off-Kultur

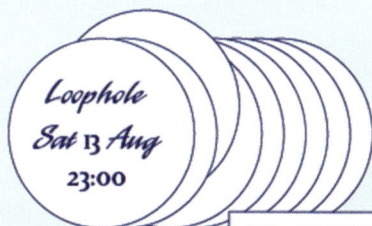

Loophole
Sat 13 Aug
23:00

OFF-KULTUR

Devon Welsh
Broshuda
S/L (DJ)

Shameless/Limitless warmly and humbly welcomes the incomparable Devon
Welsh (formerly of Majical Cloudz) for one of his premiere performances
as a solo artist.

Ambient punk — post wonk producer Broshuda (Paralaxe Editions / Sonic
Router Records) will play a special one-off weightless glambient set
as support.

Kevin Halpin

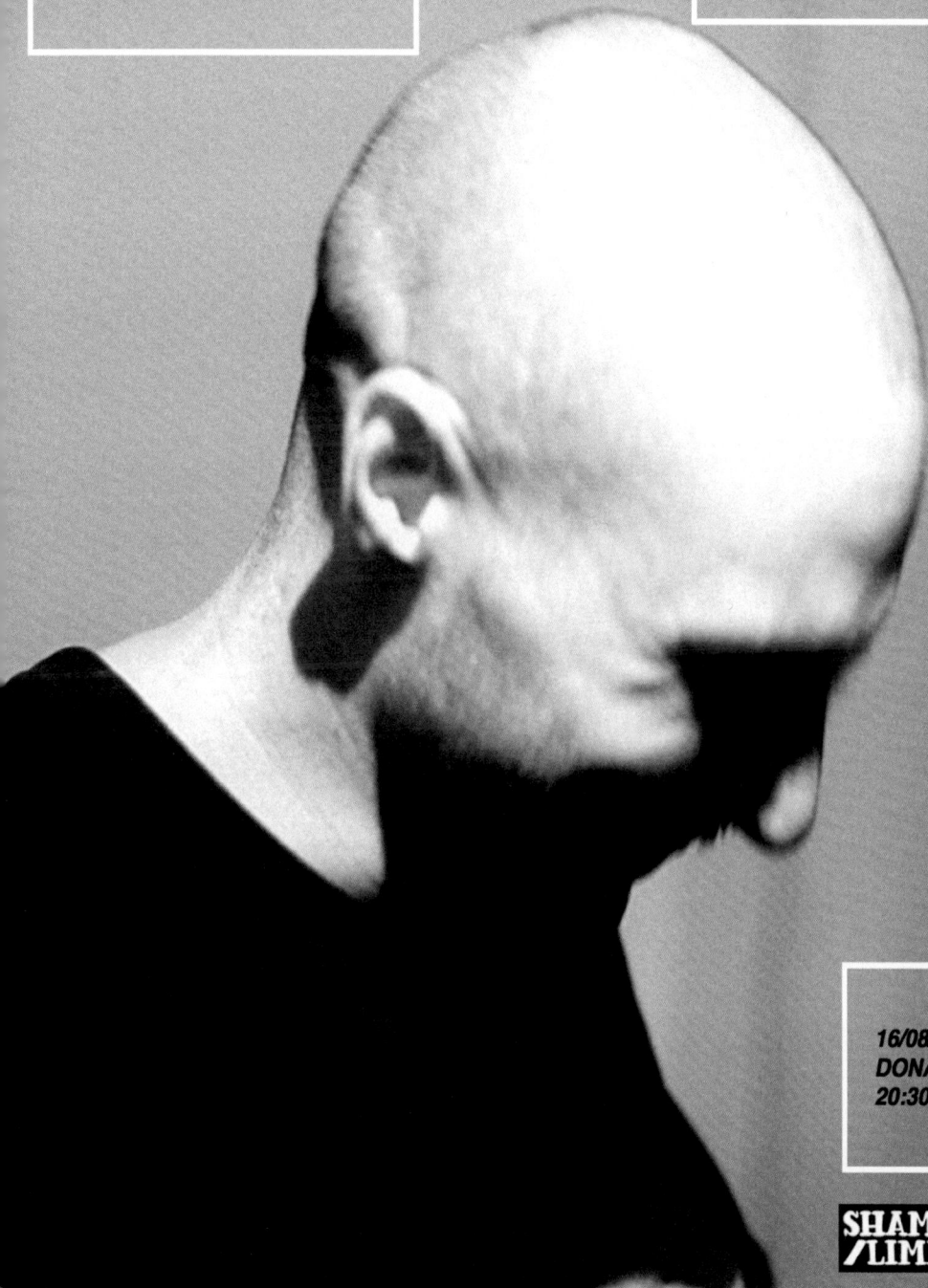

DEVON WELSH

MONTREAL

BROSHUDA

PARALAXE EDITIONS

16/08/16
DONAU 115
20:30

SHAMELESS
/LIMITLESS

2016 08 31 -   OFF-KULTUR FESTIVAL
2016 09 02
                    NEUKÖLLN

                    Various Artists

OFF-KULTUR

DONAU115

SHAMELESS LIMITLESS

FLENNEN

Das Gift

LOOPHOLE

BERLIN NEUKÖLLN

ACID ANDY / ADAM KAPLAN / ALEXANDRA BONDI DE ANTONI /
ANDRÁS / ASHIQ JAHAN KHONDKER / BASTIAN HAGEDORN /
BERLIN DISASTER / BETTER PERSON / BOBBYPIN / CASANA /
CHIKISS / CONGA FEVER / COSMO & BLACKY / DANE//CLOSE /
DARIO X / DECLAN FORDE / DUCKS! / DULAC / ERIC D. CLARK /
EYLÜL ASLAN / FRIEDE MERZ / FUNFARE / GATTO FRITTO / GIRLIE /
GRATTS / HELMUT / HUNNI'D JAWS / HUSH MOSS / IDIOTT SMITH /
JAAKKO EINO KALEVI (DJ) / JACK CHOSEF / JAMES K (DJ) /
KAPUT MAGAZINE DJ / KAROLINI / LEVENT / LINUS HALT /
LUKAS FÖHRES / MAGIC ISLAND / MAX BOSS / MIRNA BOGDANOVIC/
MOLLY NILSSON (DJ) / MONA LISA DISCO / MOON WHEEL (DJ) / NOJ /
OMEN / OMER / PHILIP FM / RINGO STARWARS / RRRKRTA /
SAM VANCE-LAW / SEAN NICHOLAS SAVAGE (DJ) / SILVIA KASTEL /
SYLVIE WEBER / TEARZ / TEREZA MUNDILOVA / TENDRE BICHE /
WATERLELYCK / WHITE LIE / YUKO YUKO / ZOZO

Mansions & Millions

NOISE KÖLLN

indie Berlin

jungle.world

KAPUT
MAGAZIN FÜR INSOLVENZ & POP

the CHOP

half-life

31.08.-02.09.2016

SAM VANCE-LAW
Artist

S/L is the first place I found a
musical community in Berlin. It
was a scene populated with your
smaller bands looking for a first
shot at a stage (that was me),
your better-known projects looking
for a guaranteed good time, and a
crowd of people knowing that if
they turned up to see an S/L gig,
they'd be part of something bigger
than a single evening.

Nothing gives you a sense of
belonging like turning up and
knowing the person on the door,
the person behind the mixing desk,
to know you don't even have to plan
with friends and they'll be there.
Long may it last and long may it
grow, cause when shows are a thing
again, I want to be there.

Lawrence Arabia
Martha Rose
Jaakko Eino Kalevi (DJ)

EMOTION MASTER AND SHAMELESS/LIMITLESS PRESENT

LAWRENCE ARABIA

+ MARTHA ROSE

+ JAAKKO EINO KALEVI AS THE DJ

AT MONSTER RONSONS

THURS 22 SEPTEMBER 20:30

Sean Nicholas Savage
Nite Jewel
Mansions and Millions (DJ)

NO FEAR
OF POP.

SHAMELESS
/LIMITLESS

PUSCHEN

NITE
JEWEL

SEAN
NICHOLAS
SAVAGE

LOS ANGELES

BERLIN

URBAN
SPREE

26
/09
/16

20
:
0
0

Skiing
Ménage à Trois
Molly Nilsson (DJ)

Shameless Limitless

Present an evening with

Skiing
(Tape Release Show!)

Ménage à trois
(Manchester)

+ Molly Nilsson (DJ)

07/10/16
West Germany
21h00

Operators
PTD
Fenster (DJ)

Shameless/Limitless proudly welcomes Operators, the ~ripping~ new analogue
post-punk project of Dan Boeckner (Wolf Parade / Divine Fits).

Support comes by way of the debut performance from PTD, a brand-new
new-age post-punk project which includes members of local go-getters
PLATTENBAU.

Fenster, true blue exemplars of "goin' good" if ever there were one,
are going to MP3 before, between and a little after the live stuff.

Paula Estévez

SHAMELESS / LIMITLESS PRESENTS...

SHAMELESS

LIMITLESS

FENSTER
DJ

PTD
EX PLATTENBAU

OPERATORS
FEAT. MEMBERS OF WOLF
PARADE & DIVINE FITS

WESTGERMANY
14/10/16   21:00

Man Duo
Aemong
Piers Martin (DJ)

Jaakko Eino Kalevi and Long-Sam have a new band.

It's called MAN DUO.

This is their first show.

Support comes courtesy of Berlin duo Aemong. Piers Martin will DJ before, between, and a little after the live stuff.

Please come.

Danielle Rahal

SHAMELESS/LIMITLESS PRESENTS...
16/10/16
MAN
DUO (JAAKKO
EINO
KALEVI
×
LONG-SAM)
+ AEMONG (BERLIN)
FIRST
SHOW!
@ MARIE-ANTOINETTE
20:30

2016 10 20   LOOPHOLE

                Vesuvio Solo
                Promise Keeper
                Better Person (DJ)

Kaspars Groševs

S/L PRESENTS

20.10.16.

VESUVIO
SOLO

BANKO GOTITI, MONTRÉAL

PROMISE
KEEPER

LONDON

LOOPHOLE

21:00

MARIE-ANTOINETTE

Aldous RH
Luka
Dallas Xanax (DJ)

ALDOUS RH
(MANCHESTER)

X
V
U
L
(BERLIN)

D
A
L
L
A
S

(IT)

X
R
N
X
X

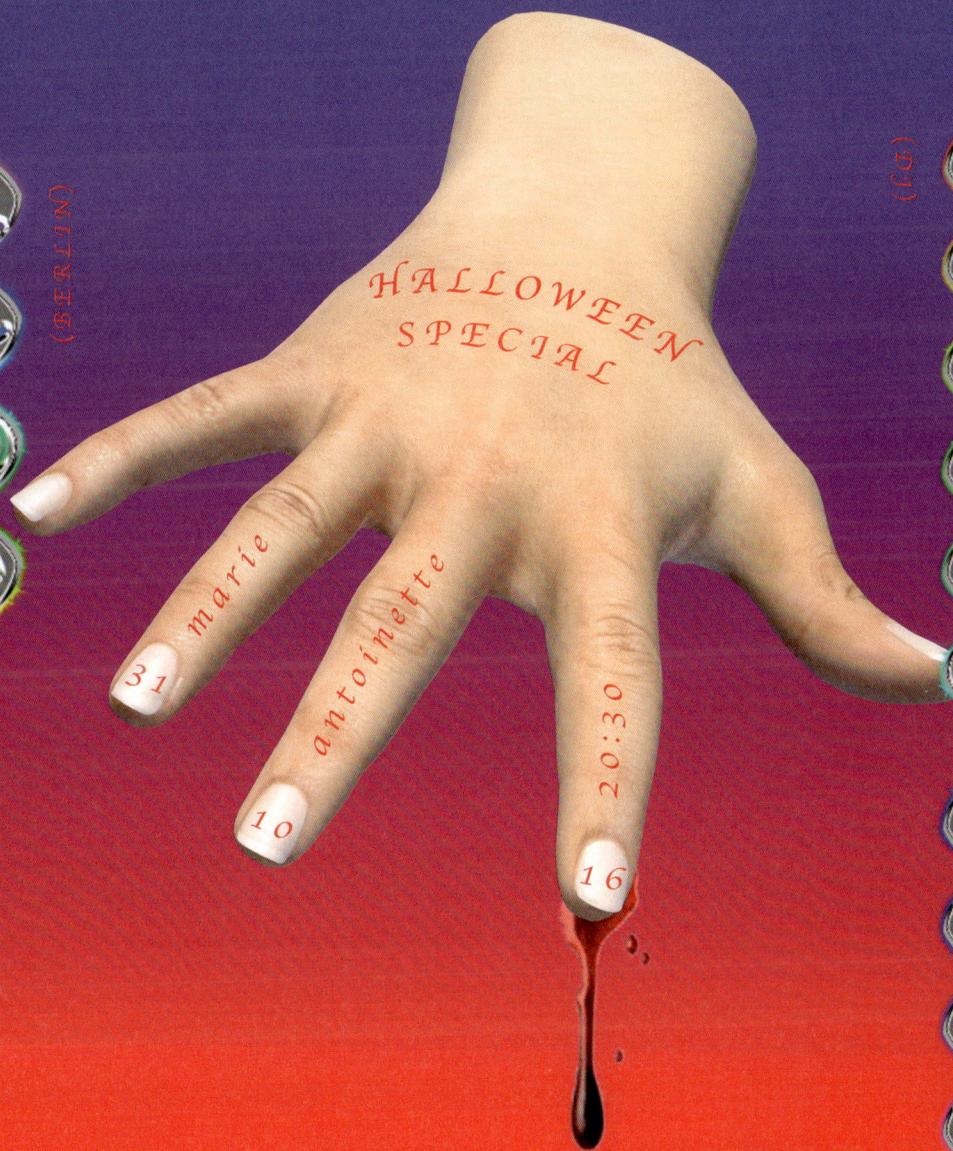

HALLOWEEN
SPECIAL

marie

antoinette

31

10

20:30

16

SHAMELESS
/LIMITLESS

2016 11 05   LOFT
              REYKJAVÍK

              Alex Cameron
              Doomsquad
              East Of My Youth
              Magic Island
              JFDR
              MX World

Gudrun Jonsdottir

Alex Cameron
Pictorial Candi

Alex Cameron and Roy Molloy are making their triumphant return to Berlin, and they'd love to play you their songs, tell you their stories, and see all your beautiful smiling faces in the flesh.

Pictorial Candi has a certain special indescribable kinda thing going on. Come see what I mean – she's playing support.

Ticket reservations are now closed. Fear not, though: a good chunk – a hefty wad, a decent serve – of tickets will be available at the door on the night. You don't need me to tell you to be punctual, do you?

Natalia Portnoy

SHAMELESS/LIMITLESS PRESENTS: 10/11/16 | 9 PM | ACUD

ALEX CAMERON
(SECRETLY CANADIAN, BERLIN)

PICTORIAL
CANDI
(MANSIONS & MILLIONS, WARSAW)

JASON HARVEY
Designer
Jayyce

I have taken some moments over the past few months to reflect on what it really means to me to "party" or to "go out" at night.

This is of course an activity that has been radically transformed by the discovery of a new respiratory virus in late 2019 (COVID-19) and still in the current moment most nightlife globally exists in a drastically reduced form due to regulations put in place to slow the current pandemic.

And you know, in some ways I don't desire to return to the old ways; there were many things wrong with the times before the virus came. But an experience I do miss is to have a small moment, where I enter a dark and poorly ventilated space w/ approx. 30 to 70 people inside, where I know that I am on some sort of "guestlist". I am allowed to enter for a full or partial reduction of regular admission price, and to take a brief reprieve from the constant alienating customer experience we all must repeat each day.

I try to believe and honour the idea that each of us on Earth is a little bit special, but if I become honest, I desire and seek out moments where I personally am made to feel like I am actually a bit more special than everyone around me. This is an experience that has been provided to me often by my friend and colleague Kevin, who runs Shameless/ Limitless, an organization for which I have designed many posters, DJ'd many parties, and attended — on the guest list, naturally — many concerts.

Project Pablo (DJ)
Molly Nilsson (DJ)
Omer (DJ)
Olga Żmiejko (DJ)

Celebrating 8 years of Shameless/Limitless.
Celebrating 8 years of given'er.
Celebrating celebration.

Come giver' good with DJs
Project Pablo (**Special 4-hour xtendamix set**), Molly Nilsson,
Omer (Cocktail d'Amore Music) and Olga Żmiejko.

Hello! please regard!

SHAMELESS /LIMITLESS
"8 year Big Big Birthday!"

presents

O shit

"DJ sets"

Project Pablo
(1080p, SOBO / Montréal)

"Special Xtendamix 4 Hour Set"

Molly Nilsson
(Dark Skies Association / Berlin)

Omer
(Cocktail D'Amore / Berlin)

Olga Żmiejk

3.12.2016

It's at **Sameheads**
"A good place to relax and DJ from computer"

VIP

California
SHIT

2017 01 31   WESTGERMANY

infinite bisous
Karolini
S/L (DJ)

DAS GIFT
AFTER PARTY

infinite bisous (DJ)

infinite bisous are putting out a new record and they're touring europe
and they're gonna have another crack at berlin and i, for one, am over
the moon.

talented (amongst other things) in the arts of songwriting, crooning and
miming, local treasure Karolini is going to play support.

early(ish) show — strict 23:00 curfew

Sharmila Banerjee

♥ INFINITE BISOUS

PRESENTED BY SHAMELESS / LIMITLESS

+ KAROLINI
(BERLIN)

(TASTY MORSELS, PARIS)

31. JAN.
2017
20:00

W E S T G E R M A N Y

+ AFTER PARTY AND INFINITE BISOUS DJ @ DAS GIFT

Pascale Project
Blanka
Mansions and Millions (DJ)

On March 22
let's all just feel good for a moment
and while we're at it
give a warm Neukölln welcome
to
our old friend
Pascale Project
and also
to first-time-in-towners
Blanka.

Just an idea.

Oh also: Mansions and Millions, fresh back from the new world, will be
disk jokering before / between and a little after the live stuff.

Strict 23:30 curfew in effect

Anna Horváth

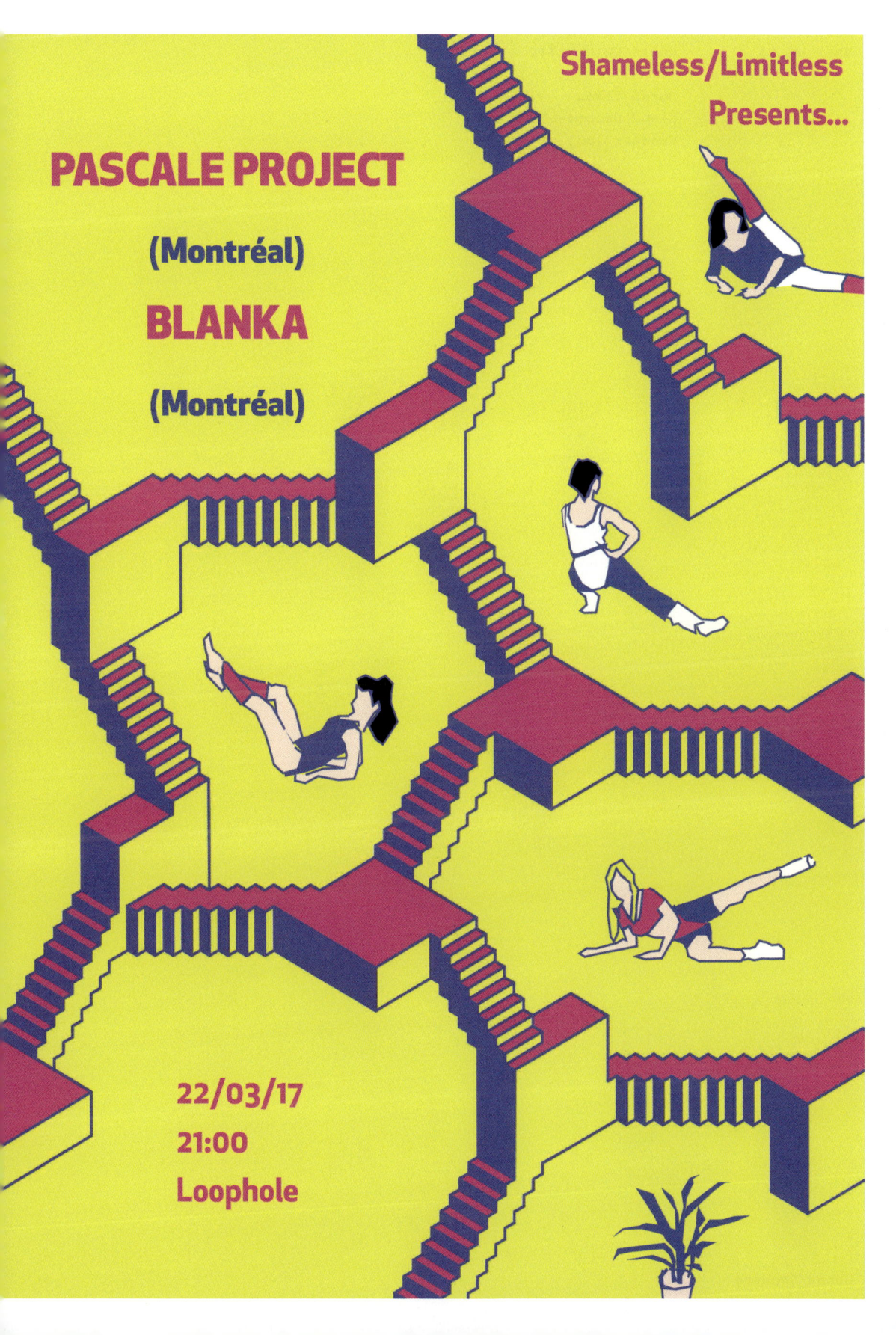

Shameless/Limitless
Presents...

PASCALE PROJECT

(Montréal)

BLANKA

(Montréal)

22/03/17

21:00

Loophole

Horse Lords
Cloud Becomes Your Hand
Fenster (DJ)

Fresh Panties and Shameless/Limitless present

HORSE LORDS
(Baltimore)

**CLOUD BECOMES
YOUR HAND**
(Brooklyn)

+ FENSTER (DJ)

**APRIL 14TH - 21H00
MARIE ANTOINETTE**

Cindy Lee
Omen
Stromboli

Marianna Ostrowska

CINDY LEE

(ex Women, Calgary)

OMEN

(Berlin)

ACUD
29/04/17
20:00

Jack Ladder
Seb
S/L (DJ)

IN A DRAMATIC TURN OF EVENTS
A LAST-MINUTE BOOKING FOR THE AGES
REPRESENTING THE BERLIN COMPLETION OF THE TRIFECTA OF SYDNEY'S FINEST
THE ONE AND ONLY
JACK LADDER
WILL BE PLAYING ON MAY 15 AT INTERNET EXPLORER.

Seb will be playing support. Sebheads rejoice.

Tell yr m9s. This is an all-caps kinda thing.

I E is the hot new spot in tief NK. Aks around if ye gots to.

Kevin Halpin

15/05/17
SHAMELESS/LIMITLESS PRESENTS...

JACK
LADDER
(SYDNEY)

+
SEB
(BERLIN)

20:00@@@INTERNET EXPLORER@@@20:00
20:00@@@INTERNET EXPLORER@@@20:00

Molly Nilsson
Dubais
Skiing
Jaakko Eino Kalevi (DJ)

Sold Out
No tickets available at the door.
Thank you!

Big dreamers that they are, Dark Skies Association and Shameless/Limitless
are thrilled to present Molly Nilsson, live in concert in celebration of
the release of her 8th LP, Imaginations. The show will take place at the
newly and beautifully reconstituted Festsaal Kreuzberg, with support via
arabpop futurist DUBAIS and local favourite Skiing. Jaakko Eino Kalevi
will DJ throughout the night.

Jason Harvey

Imaginations

23 MAY 2017 FESTSAAL KREUZBERG - BERLIN
24 MAY 2017 UT CONNEWITZ - LEIPZIG

DARK SKIES ASSOCIATION

SHAMELESS
/LIMITLESS

Alex Cameron
Helen Fry

LOOPHOLE
AFTER PARTY

Alex Cameron (DJ)
Roy Molloy (DJ)
Helen Fry (DJ)
Karolini (DJ)

It's Friday night in the big smoke and Bondi Beach's Pajero king is in town and we're all entitled to roll fast and loose when the occasion calls and if it weren't already clear the phone's ringing it's Herr Occash on the other end and he's sayin' "Carpe the party, baby" and so the real question then is: u cool to carpe? Looks plain as day to me that everyone else is c2c. And so that's what we're gonna do. We're gonna have a party. Recently minted 10000+ Likes title holder (not to mention Urban Spree headliner) Alex Cameron is going to DJ. The unstoppable Helen Fry is going to DJ. Roy Molloy on horn is going to DJ. Karolini from the neighbourhood is going to DJ. Chances are some kind of special guests are gonna DJ too, but you leave that to me to figure out.

Natalia Portnoy

Oscar Key Sung
LIA LIA
Magic Island (DJ)

~It's a beautiful lyfe~

Shameless/Limitless proudly presents

Melbourne's resident club heartbreaker Oscar Key Sung,
freshly minted Berliner and budding pop iconoclast LIA LIA
+ Neukölln resident raconteur Magic Island on MP3s throughout.

All IRL AFK 4 U 'n I @ I E.

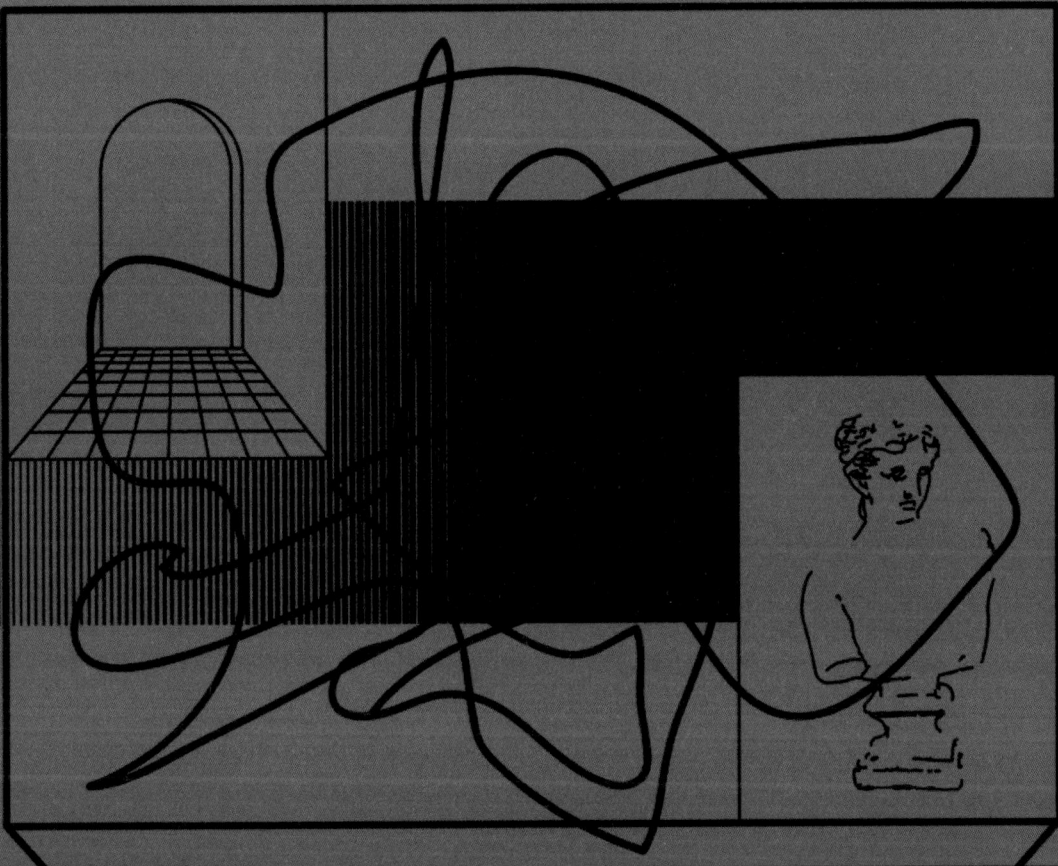

29 / 06 / 17
Shameless/Limitless Presents...

LINEUP

Oscar Key Sung	(Melbourne)
Lia Lia	(Berlin)
Magic Island	(DJ)

21:00 @INTERNET EXPLORER

TABITHA SWANSON
Designer

Working with S/L has always been
a very free and fun experience.

When I first moved to Berlin and
wanted to contribute to the DIY
music scene, S/L took lil ol' me
in and were really trusting with
giving me creative freedom. Since
then, we've worked together on a
number of events.

Because of the continued creative
freedom and trust, it's always
enabled and catalysed an outpour
of many ideas. I've often
contributed a lot of different
concepts at once, simply because
they came forth.

Windows 98 (DJ)
Molly Nilsson (DJ)
Linda Lee (DJ)
S/L (DJ)

Shameless/Limitless proudly presents
a summer's night of Everything Now
spread over the grounds of ACUD
with DJs

Windows 98 (Win Butler of Arcade Fire)
Molly Nilsson
Linda Lee (Berlin Community Radio)
+ maybe some surprises too.

Limited capacity — plan accordingly.

02 07 17

ACUD MACHT NEU

SHAMELESS LIMITLESS

22:00

WITH DJ SETS BY

WINDOWS 98
(WIN BUTLER OF ARCADE FIRE)

MOLLY NILSSON

LINDA LEE
(BERLIN COMMUNITY RADIO)

VETERANENSTR. 21
10119 BERLIN

Sean Nicholas Savage
Calvin Love
Pictorial Candi (DJ)

That we — that's you, that's me, that's us — are in a position to bear
witness to a performance on a Friday night at the peak of summer from a
talent as singular and indomitable as the legend in the making that is
Sean Nicholas Savage is something that we should collectively take stock
of, and subsequently celebrate by way of making a ticket reservations THIS
VERY INSTANT by mailing your particulars to shamelesslimitless@gmail.com.

Support comes in the form of Calvin Love, another noteworthy talent from
the deep pool of excellence that Edmonton, Alberta has provided us with.

Needless to say, ~excitement runneth high~

DOUBLE WHAMMY CONCERT

Shameless Limitless Presents
SEAN NICHOLAS SAVAGE
CALVIN LOVE
10 EURO
9pm friday july 21st 2017
at Marie-Antoinette

Molly Nilsson
The Beat Escape

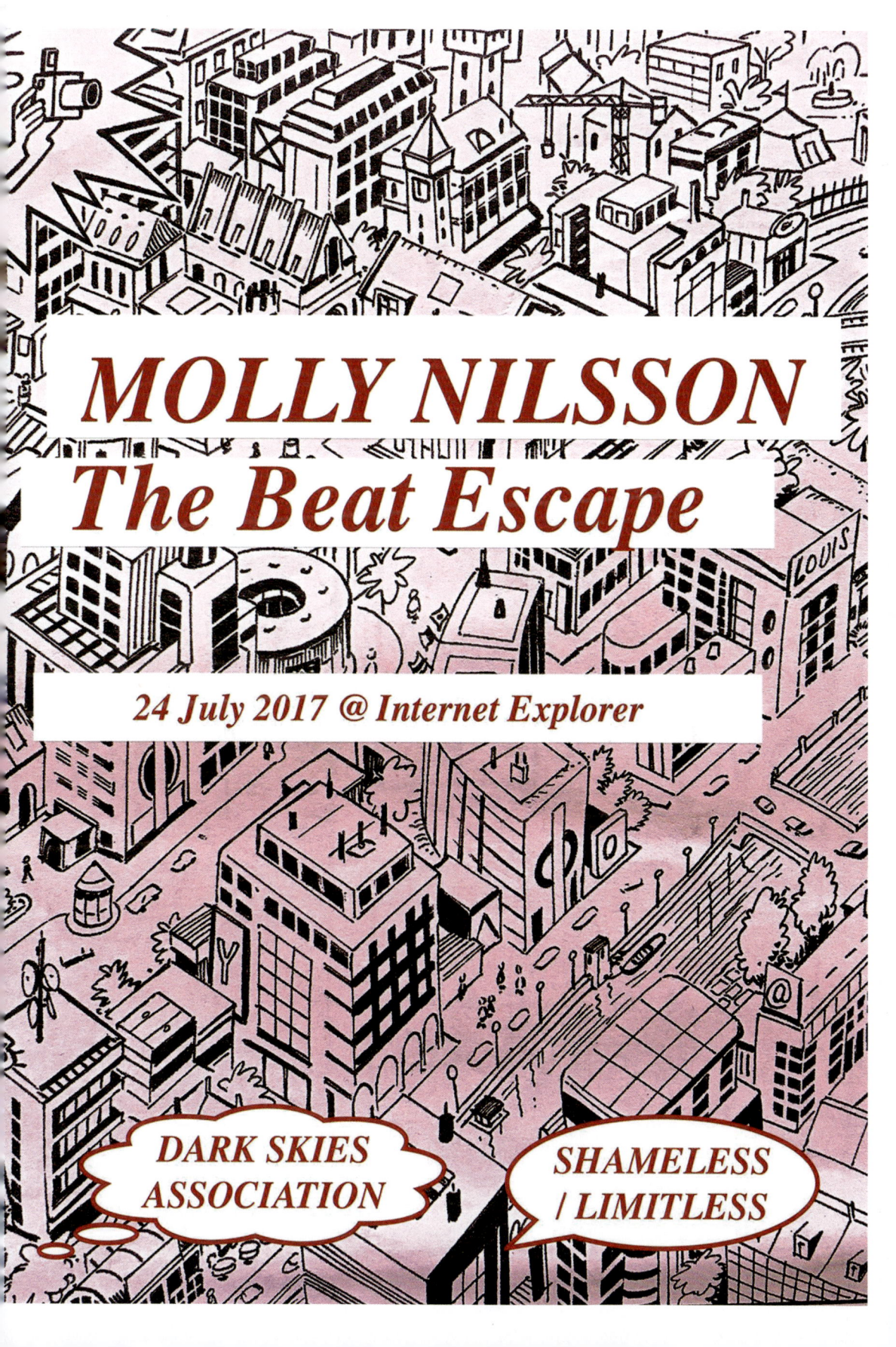

MOLLY NILSSON

The Beat Escape

24 July 2017 @ Internet Explorer

DARK SKIES ASSOCIATION

SHAMELESS / LIMITLESS

Better Person
Bad Hammer
Karolini

On the evening of August 11, 2017,
and on the occasion of another beautiful night of being alive,
Shameless/Limitless + Mansions and Millions proudly present

– Better Person
Neukölln's crooning crown prince of "it's complicated", fresh off an
exceptionally busy run of support slots with the likes of heavy hitters
TOPS, Alex Cameron, and Roosevelt, is playing an all-too-rare homekiez
show. Your wholehearted, respectful, and enthusiastic engagement will
be reciprocated fivefold. Worth every złoty.

– Bad Hammer

– Karolini

Ticket reservations at shamelesslimitless@gmail.com.

Mansions
&Millions
SHAMELESS
/LIMITLESS
KAROLINI
BAD HAMMER
BETTER PERSON
INTERNET EXPLORER | AUGUST 11TH | 21:00

Kool A.D.
Cult Days
Weekend Money
Heimer (DJ)

SHAMELESS/LIMITLESS
PRESENTS

KOOL
A.D. [EX DAS RACIST]
CULT
DAYS

14.09./21:00 ACUD

Better Person (DJ)
Butterfly Hour aka StarRhi Cowboy (DJ)
Helen Fry (DJ)
Karolini (DJ)
Molly Nilsson (DJ)
S/L (DJ)
Sean Nicholas Savage (DJ)
Skiing (DJ)

~Ashes to ashes, dust to dust, life is too short so party we must~

On the night of Friday, September 15, please join DJs
Better Person
Butterfly Hour aka StarRhi Cowboy
Helen Fry
Karolini
Molly Nilsson
Sean Nicholas Savage
Shameless/Limitless
Skiing

And the good people of the DIY Neukölln music community at large as we
toast Jan and Matthias, the unsung heroes who have run our beloved Loophole
Berlin for years on end, asking only that we have a good time, that we STFU
on the sidewalk, and that we don't mind the mess (toilets will be fixed
soon I promise).

While the future of the venue remains unknown, let's take this opportunity
to revel in the fact of its very existence. Its glorious, glorious existence.

All proceeds on the night will go to the house. Even so, tip yr bartender,
and for god's sake, no Späti beers.

Jason Harvey

Shameless Limitless x Loophole

"time 2 face the music"

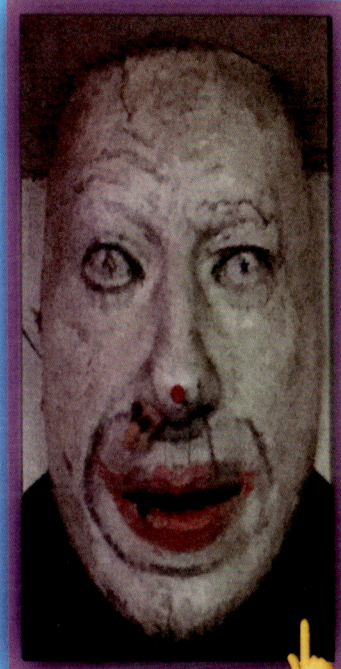

W/ DJs

- Better Person
- Butterfly Hour
- Helen Fry
- Karolini
- Molly Nilsson
- S/L
- Sean Nicholas Savage
- Skïing

Ancient "Loophole Jester mask" photographed in mid-2107
date of production unknown

Bye

15/09/17

22:00 - End

Kirin J Callinan
Bea1991
S/L (DJ)

KIRIN J. CALLINAN

SUPPORT: BEA1991

01.10. BERLIN
KANTINE AM BERGHAIN

kirinjcallinan.com   facebook.com/KirinJCallinan
meltbooking.com   facebook.com/wearemeltbooking

SHAMELESS
LIMITLESS

MELT!
BOOKING

Man Duo
Wet Love$$
Helen Fry (DJ)

Indoor Music and Drinks — that's the Mother of the Unicorn promo wing for
those unaware — and Shameless/Limitless exchanged some thoughtful emails,
bantered mindfully over messenger and even had an IRL sesh or two to
put together a happening which will, inshallah, satisfy the punter, pay
the promoters and further solidify the already unfuckwithably positive
reputations of performers MAN DUO (a new men's duo featuring Jaakko Eino
Kalevi and Long-Sam), Wet Love$$ and DJ Helen Fry.

We've done our part so now it's on you to do yours. Pay the cover, party
like you mean it, and tip your bartender, please and thanks.

This is a Chop Chip show, which is to say that if you are a holder of a
Chop Chip you will pay reduced entry.

Joe Kelly

INDOOR MUSIC & DRINKS
+
SHAMELESS/LIMITLESS
present

- MAN DUO -

+

WET LOVE$$

+

Helen Fry (DJ)

@INTERNET EXPLORER
05.10.17 | 21:00

Molly Nilsson
Ménage à Trois
Vraiment Nice (DJ)
Butterfly Hour (DJ)
S/L (DJ)

Shameless/Limitless Presents:

MOLLY NILSSON

(Berlin)

MÉNAGE À TROIS

(Manchester)

+DJs   Vraiment Nice   Butterfly Hour   @Westgermany   23:30

Bad Hammer
Baal & Mortimer

S/L proudly presents
a twofer of local excellence
doing the neighbourhood proud:
Bad Hammer
and
Baal & Mortimer
live, in concert, for your enjoyment.

Please come.

Johannes Badzura

shameless/limitless
presents

BAD HAMMER
BAAL & MORTIMER
26/10/2017
loophole/21:00

STEPHANIE HAMER
Designer
Door Staff

I'd heard about "one of those Shameless/
Limitless nights" long before I started
working the door there.

My eventual initiation was THAT Alex Cameron
night, and no matter how blurry that event, or
any others (losing my mind dancing to No Drama
and Magic Island DJ sets at Internet Explorer,
being chased around Boddinstraße by a man with
a mink shawl after a Loophoole show) have
been, the image I hold of an S/L experience
is that of dancing to a weird and wonderful
soundtrack with friends old and new.

Though most memories of my favourite nights
are hazy, my first introduction to S/L is not,
and it was probably the most inspirational:
the "9 Years S/L Poster Retrospective" at Das
Giftraum, in Dec 2017. As a visual artist who
was a newbie to Berlin, I had a field day
lapping up all the cool AF artwork, writing
down the musicians, bands, artists and venues.
It felt like the first proper gateway into the
city and still continues to be an absolute
goldmine of discovery for me. Long live S/L!

Geneva Jacuzzi
A Tribute To February Montaine
DJ Joshy

SHAMELESS/LIMITLESS PRESENTS...

GENEVA JACUZZI

(LOS ANGELES)

PLUS GUESTS

A TRIBUTE
TO FEBRUARY
MONTAINE
(BERLIN)

28/10/2017

WESTGERMANY

21:00

Marker Starling
Nicholas Krgovich
Fenster (DJ)

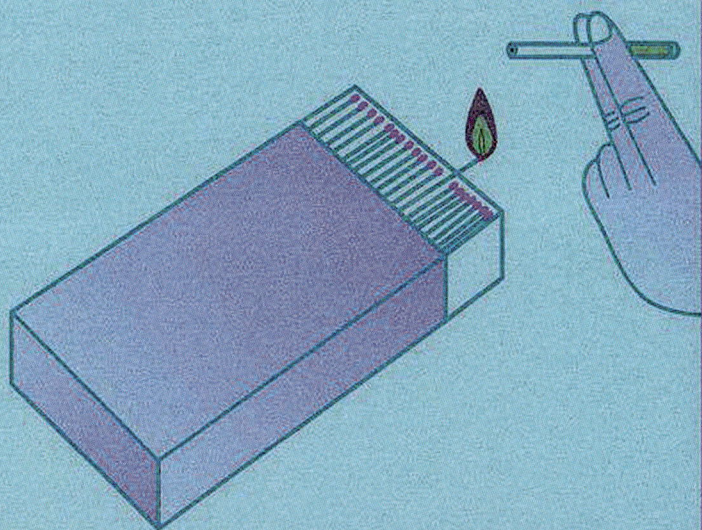

Tonstartssbandht
Aemong

TONSTARTSSBANDHT

Westgermany

04.11.17

20:00

TONSTARTSSBANDHT + GUESTS

(Mexican Summer, Orlando)

2017 11 05   ACUD MACHT NEU

                FAKA
                Handjerks
                Weeeirdos (DJ)

SHAMELESS/LIMITLESS PRESENTS

FAKA

05.11.17
ACUD

with
HANDJERKS   20:00   + DJ
                                               WEEEIRDOS

Honey Harper
Seb

Honey Harper

07.11.

BERLIN, LOOPHOLE
SUPPORT: SEB

facebook.com/HONEYHARPER1
meltbooking.com   facebook.com/wearemeltbooking

SHAMELESS LIMITLESS

MELT! BOOKING

2017 11 08   URBAN SPREE
                    MAC DEMARCO AFTER PARTY

                    Butterfly Hour (DJ)
                    Karolini (DJ)
                    Ken Chic (DJ)
                    Surprise Guest DJs

Jason Harvey

Hello weary traveller!

Please! Cum'st ye to a hot and 100%
Official state sanctioned
"MAC DEMARCO CONCERT
AFTERPARTY"

happening immediately after literal
Mac Demarco Concert in local area

Please come and try to enjoy DJ music sel
of rock and other types of music from
MAC???* JOE?** JON????***

and additional professional quality DJ'ing from local artists
"Karolini" and "Butterfly Hour"

** Also full bathroom privilge (liquid and solid)
reliable access to cell phone network
and literally thousands of other surprises
which await you ;)

"Urban Spree
Wednesday, Nove 8th, 2017
99 Revaler Str.

2017 11 11   INTERNET EXPLORER
                  TOPS AFTER PARTY

                  TOPS (DJ)
                  Antoine93
                  Fenster (DJ)
                  Jason Harvey (DJ)

Following the band's triumphant return to a Berlin stage, TOPS are going
to head across town to Internet Explorer to goof off, play MP3s, and
bask in the glow of all the friendlies that showed up to be there to do
the very same thing. Fenster and Jason Harvey on tunes, too.

ONE-TIME BONUS OFFER
Fellow Montrealer Antoine93, who will be touring in support of his
debut LP, is going to play live! All the hits + a surprise or two for
the A93 heads.

Martin Dziallas

Farao
Jae Tyler

JAE TYLER! + FARAO

STREET PULSE

SHAMELESS LIMITLESS

Alex Cameron
Briana Marela
S/L (DJ)

THE ALCAM

ALEX CAMERON:
HOME
AGAIN

ROY: I WAS A FORCED WITNESS

* LIDO BERLIN
* NOVEMBER 20
* HEADLINE SHOW
* TICKETS NOW!
* SPECIAL GUESTS

www.greyzone-tickets.de

Blue Hawaii
LINNÉA (DJ)
RIP Swirl (DJ)
Deadlift (DJ)

Aisha Franz

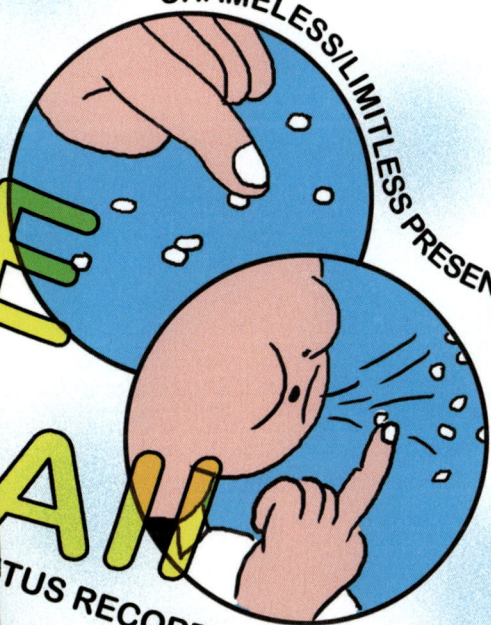

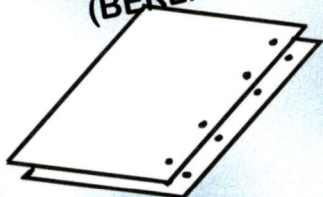

AISHA FRANZ
Designer

Making artwork for something music-related
might be every designer's wet dream.
Something magical happens when combining
images with music, be it on a record cover
or gig poster — it just makes BOOM!

Shameless/Limitless manages to connect
not only musicians but a whole like-minded
community based in and around Neukölln
whose aesthetics speak to each other.

While sitting on one end sampling sketches
and drawings and colours at the computer,
I can feel the connection to the person at
the other end sampling sounds and beats
and chords and dance moves inside a smoky,
crowded and ecstatic hole of a DIY space.

               Roy Molloy (DJ)
               TOPS (DJ)
               Jaakko Eino Kalevi (DJ)
               Linda Lee (DJ)
               Vraiment Nice (DJ)
               Alex Cameron (DJ, Cancelled)

Celebrating 9 Years of Shameless/Limitless,
soundtracked by musical selections courtesy of DJs

Roy Molloy (Alex Cameron's Business Partner and Sax Man, Secretly
Canadian, Sydney),
TOPS (Arbutus, Montréal),
Jaakko Eino Kalevi (Weird World, Berlin),
Linda Lee (Berlin Community Radio)
and
Vraiment Nice (Berlin)

All DJ sets

Alas, owing to unforeseen circumstances, Sameheads will no longer be
playing host to this happening. Additionally, Alex Cameron has come up
against a hard-charging wisdom tooth situation, so he's out and
Roy Molloy is stepping in to save the day.

Praise be to Internet Explorer for welcoming S/L for this, the venue's
final event before closing for hibernation until spring 2018.

Please come!

Norman Palm

Norman,

right off the bat: it's a real deal nice thing for you to be making another poster for S/L - thanks very much for doing this! Given the budget, I'm aware that this is firmly in the category of passion project for you. Thanks for caring ⦚

Pardon the cut and paste nature (i.e. the content being pretty similar to what I have sent through to designers in the past) of this mail. I seem to have found an effective formula for communicating with designers, so I'm sticking with it.

I'm hoping that you'll find everything you need for the poster here. If you have any questions / thoughts, don't hesitate to ask.

Compensation for the poster will consist of 50 euros cash, 2 guest list spots for the party and all the www shout outs I can muster. You'll also get a hard copy (or 3) of the poster fer yr archives.

Some things to consider:

-please make the design vertical as opposed to horizontal. I'm looking for a poster design, as opposed to just an FB cover image design, so please make it A3 - 42.2 x 29.9 cm for print from flyeralarm. If for whatever reason you want to additionally make an FB event image that matches the poster design, they are sized 524 x 1000 pixels. Please also send over an instagram sized version of the finished poster - size 709 x 886.

-Please continue to mind this old chestnut: do not make a horse / unicorn / horses / unicorns the central theme of the poster. Somehow many people have opted to do that in the past, and I don't want to be the horse poster guy. Don't get me wrong, i like horses fine, just, you know, enough's enough.

-Please include the following text. It is presented below for ease of legibility for you, but feel free to change it up (i.e. put the date at the bottom) if you prefer. Also feel free to play around with all caps / no caps / placement on the poster / etc.

09/12/17
9 Years of Shameless/Limitless
With DJs
Alex Cameron (Secretly Canadian, Sydney)
TOPS (Arbutus, Montréal)
Linda Lee (Berlin Community Radio)
Vraiment Nice (Berlin)
23:00
Internet Explorer
+ Shameless/Limitless Poster Retrospective,
Opening 08/12/17 @ Das Giftraum

-Owing to, shall we say, unforeseen circumstances, I've had to pull a late-game venue change, from the initially announced Sameheads to Internet Explorer. That being the case, please put an extra emphasis on highlighting that the party is happening at IE. Leave any mention of Sameheads off; I'll communicate the change of plans through other channels.

-I find the wording re: the addition of the exhibition to be somewhat clunky. Perhaps you can dream up a more elegant way of getting that info on the poster?

I'm intentionally leaving the venue address off. If people don't know where it is they can google it easily enough.

As far as notes on art direction go, here's where I'm at: given that I'm shelling out for some big(ish) acts, and since this party is ostensibly about celebrating the Shameless/Limitless entity, I would like to have the names be more (rather than less) central to the overall design.

I don't really have much in the way of art direction to provide beyond that, either than to ask that you please take a minute to consider the tone of the artists in specific and Shameless/Limitless posters in general (archives of which can be found at my FB) and to aim for something that generally fits the feel of the happening. It has happened the odd time in the past that a poster comes in that is totally off vibe, and that's not good for anyone.

Re: yr riso print idea. I'm v much up for interesting / out of the ordinary ways of getting the word out, provided, of course, that it doesn't break the budget. I feel like 50 euros printing budget is appropriate for this. I'm hoping to get 500 copies printed. If you have something in mind that comes in a little over that Im flexible and open to ideas.

Unless you hear otherwise from me in the next few hours, we can consider this information to be final. As ever, I'll aim to answer/address any questions / thoughts / big point ideas as they come up, busy schedule be damned.

Thanks again, and looking seeing the final product!

Kevin

Soft as Snow
Kelora
Phil FM (DJ)
Ken Chic (DJ)
S/L (DJ)

Shameless/Limitless presents
in the sense that this is a gift
from S/L to you
because it is
very much something to hold dear
and to cherish
and to anticipate and remember
(though, that said, you still gotta put up some bread for it,
so I suppose we can also just think of this as a transaction
if you're gonna be precious about it)

Soft as Snow (Houndstooth, Berlin — premiering brand-new material in
advance of the release of their forthcoming debut LP, out April 6)
Kelora (Glasgow — Berlin debut)
+ DJs
Phil FM (Berlin Community Radio)
Ken Chic
and
for the early slot
S/L.

Tabitha Swanson

17/02/18 —————— 22:00

Loophole

Shameless/Limitless Presents....
Soft As Snow (Houndstooth, Berlin)
Kelora (Glasgow)
+ DJs
Phil FM (Berlin Community Radio)
Ken Chic (Berlin)
S/L

Grand Prix
Henrich Ferdinand Jelínek
Magic Island (DJ)

O shit — another rad happening at Loophole which is destined to read well
in the eventual oral history of relevant Neukölln nights out, featuring:

Grand Prix (Copenhagen, Berlin debut!)
Henrich Ferdinand Jelínek (First show!)
Magic Island (DJ)

It'll be cool I think please come.

21|02|18

20:30h

GRAND PRIX
(CΩPΞΠHΛGΣN)

HENRICH F. JΣLINEK
(BΣRLIN)

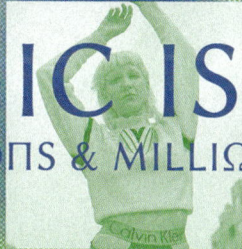

MΔGIC ISLΛND
(DJ, MΛNSIΘΠS & MILLIΩNS, BΣRLIN)

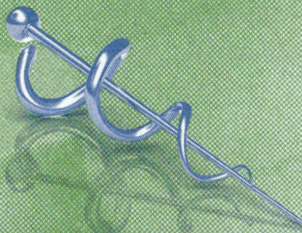

LΘΘPHΩLE

Sam Vance-Law
Educated Body (DJ)
S/L (DJ)

SAM VANCE-LAW
HOMOTOPIA
RECORD RELEASE CONCERT & PARTY
SAT, MARCH 03 2018
PRACHTWERK BERLIN

WWW.SAMVANCELAW.COM
PAINTING BY NORBERT BISKY

Marcin Masecki
Wet Love$$

Feels something approaching sublime to be welcomed back at reconstituted
Neukölln institution Donau115 for a show with two of the most talented
cats in the neighbourhood: pre-eminent pianist Marcin Masecki and
freewheelin' sax – dub experimentalist Wet Love$$.

Show some respect – dress nice, tip your bartender, say nice things.

Please note that this is a relatively early show – doors at 19:30, Wet
Love$$ will play at 20:30, Marcin at some undefined point thereafter.

Elke Foltz

Shameless/ Limitless

presents...

MARCIN MASECKI *(Berlin)*
WET LOVE$$ *(Berlin)*

07/03/18
20:30
Donau 115

Omer (DJ)
Dan Yal (DJ)
James Booth (DJ)
Maya Postepski (DJ)
Yha Yha (DJ)
S/L (DJ)

B U D S

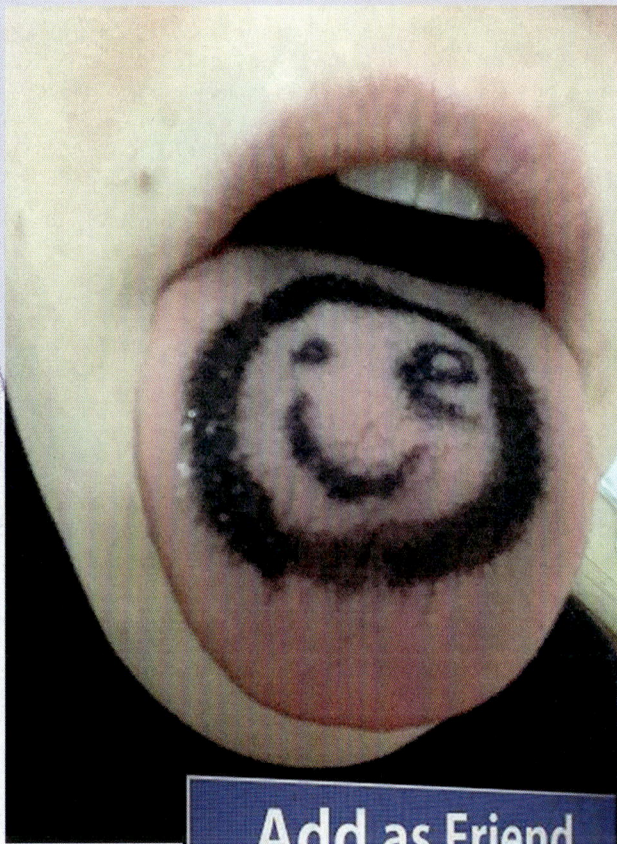

shameless/limitless x weeeirdos

OMER
(cocktail d'amore/love on the rocks)
JAMES BOOTH
(growing bin/weeeirdos)
MAYA POSTEPSKI
(of tr/st/brussels)
YHA YHA
(new world dysorder/berlin)
DAN YAL
(weeeirdos)
S/L
(shameless/limitless)

23:00

@ INTERNET EXPLORER   **MARCH 17th 2018**

Holiday Sidewinder
GRIP TIGHT
Panni Simai (DJ)

Holiday Sidewinder fanclub members rejoice: the celebrated Sydneysider
singer-songwriter (not to mention ex Bridezilla frontperson and current
Alex Cameron keyboardist) is making her Berlin debut, and it is going
to be something akin to delightful.

New dude on the block GRIP TIGHT is playing support.

Panni Simai on pitch-perfect MP3s before, between, and after.

Hugh Faulkner

20/03/18

Shameless/Limitless Presents...

Holliday Sidewinder
(Sydney)

GRIP TIGHT (Berlin)
20:30
LOOPHOLE

Phèdre
Jinka
OGQT
No_Drama (DJ)
S/L (DJ)

Sebastian Dürer

Shameless / Limitless

presents...

Phèdre (Toronto)

Jinka (Berlin)

DJ

OGQT (Toronto)

No Drama Berlin

S/L

24/03/18

Loophole 22°°

OK

What the hell does it take to destroy a pink blob of joy? What the hell does it take to destroy a pink blob of joy? What the hell does it take to destroy a pink
blob...

fake spraycan artisanal font poster by xxs

WESTGERMANY

Le Villejuif Underground
Saba Lou & Oska Wald
Simon Wojan (DJ)

Oska Wald

DAVE BIDDLE
Linda Fox
© Linda Fox

In 2018, a grown man living in Vancouver, Canada made an album in his bedroom under the pseudonym © Linda Fox. After shopping his new sounds around town and getting little interest from confused Canadian media outlets, he decided to test the European Market. He'd heard about a booker in Berlin going by the name Shameless/Limitless, so he fired off a message on Facebook. Being a grown man and being from Canada, he had little hope that the stranger in Berlin would respond at all.

Now, to tell you the truth, I am that full-grown Canadian man, and to find that original FB message I had to scroll back through a thread now containing hundreds of casual chats, complex marketing strategies, international photo ops, video clips from live sets and links to old Can-Con alt-rock gems. Going back through that three-year messenger thread reminded me that two grown men can form a beautiful friendship no matter how fully grown they are. And that's the point of little DIY music communities, isn't it? It's not to get famous, it's to form beautiful friendships with other grown men.

Making art really only feels satisfying if the art finds a home. I'm fortunate that the art that I make found a home in such a welcoming and supportive scene thousands of miles away from Vancouver, in Neukölln. To quote the man himself, "It ain't often that a cold email leads to what we've got goin' on." But what exactly is goin' on? Well, since sending that cold email I've become an outsider on the inside of a really nice world made up of people like JJ, Seb, Candi, Johannes, Lisa, Ryan, Billy, Alex and Kari (to name a few)… an endless list of humble stars dancing together through a galaxy of sweaty shows. And if you zoom out on all those stars, you'll see they form a constellation that spells out two simple letters: S/L.

Linda Fox
slimgirl fat aka ugly dragon
Zen Xen (DJ)

Rare is the occasion that a convergence of happenings as intriguing and
ticket purchase-worthy as this comes together. I mean, who knows, probably
in the greater cosmos weird amazing shit happens all the time, but I'm
talking about our plane of music and clubs and kunst and the like.

Let me explain: unsolicited note from far-out newcomer Vancouver project
Linda Fox piques significant interest and repeated streams MEANWHILE
slimgirl fat aka ugly dragon sends over but a single MP3, one that is
strong enough to generate an urge to book happening asap MEANWHILE a
trusted insider whispers in my ear that there's a new venue in town
and it's objectively a wonderful space they're DTF and tickety boom,
here we are, all going to the show on May 8 at a new spot called Darwin
(immediately next door to Marie-Antoinette — I guess that makes it
Holzmarktstraße 15-18) with Linda Fox and slimgirl fat aka ugly dragon.

Zen Xen (NO DISK) will DJ before / between / after.

Goes w/o saying: please come.

Julia Kidder

08/05/18

Shameless / Limitless
Presents...

Linda Fox (Vancouver)
Slimgirl Fat (Berlin)

20:30
Darwin

John Moods backed by The Hole Boys
Pictorial Candi
DJ Animaciòn

Aisha Franz

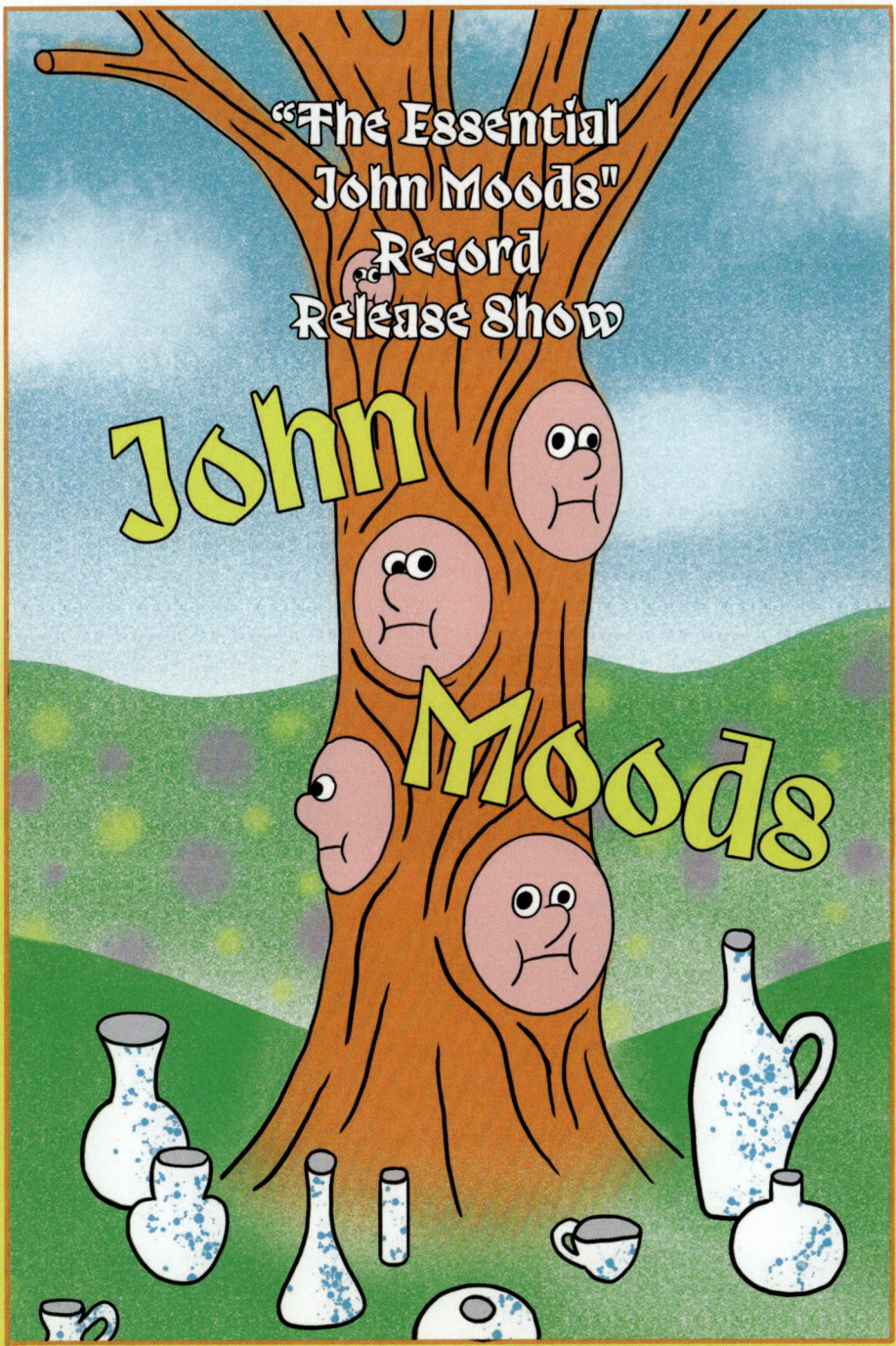

Tim Koh
CMON
DJ Scheisse

Shameless/Limitless proudly presents the Berlin debut of two very new
and very legit and very relaxed and also v rad musical undertakings: Tim
Koh (longtime bass player in Ariel Pink's Haunted Graffiti + collaborator
to the stars, including Gang Gang Dance, Connan Mockasin, Prince Rama,
Kirin J Callinan, etc etc) & CMON, a new band which trades in a type of
tunage best described as sounding like it emanates from a confusing mix
of nations, and which also includes 2/3rds of Regal Degal.

DJ Scheisse will dj scheisse before, between and after.

Steffen Ullmann

Shameless/Limitless
Presents...

Tim Koh
(of Ariel Pink's
Haunted Graffiti)

CMON
(Los Angeles)

20/05/2018, 20h
@ Internet Explorer

2018 07 07   INTERNET EXPLORER
                  NYEGE NYEGE TAPES SHOWCASE

                  Otim Alpha
                  Sounds Of Sisso
                  TOPS (DJ)
                  Ross Alexander (DJ)

07/07/18
23:00
INTERNET EXPLORER
SOUNDS OF SISSO
(DAR ES SALAAM)
NYEGE
NYEGE
TAPES
SHOWCASE
OTIM ALPHA
(GULU CITY)
DJ SETS BY
TOPS
(ARBUTUS)
ROSS ALEXANDER
(DISCREPANT)
THE CHOP
SHAMELESS
LIMITLESS

Donny Benét
Doris
S/L (DJ)

Chalk up another tally on the "Aussies 2 Watch Watch List", 'cos S/L
is brining thee Donny Benét (who's also a player in Jack Ladder's
Dreamlanders) to Berlin for a Loophole happening which promises to be
hotter than a south Bondi sauna.

Stating that Doris, the solo project of Andreya of Gurr, is going to be
playing an #ultrarare set to open the show makes me feel like I'm doing
a real good job of this booking thing.

Please come.

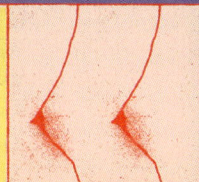

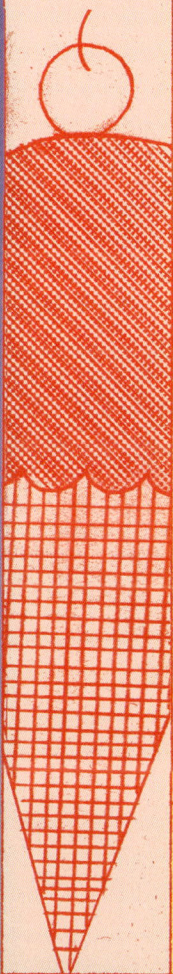

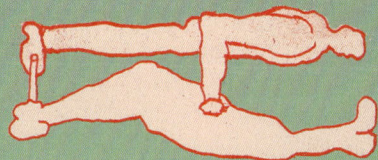

Bea1991
Karel
Raven Artson
Ty-Tas (DJ)

Following the unequivocally positive life experience in which Amsterdam-
based promoters, publishers & wonderful people Subbacultcha welcomed S/L
to their town, it is with a certain and significant level of excitement
that the favour is now being returned, with Subbacultcha presenting
a lineup of XXX favs at Internet Explorer:

With:
Bea1991
Karel
Raven Artson
Tv-Tas DJ before / between / after.

Rebecca Martin

SUBBACULTCHA X SHAMELESS/LIMITLESS

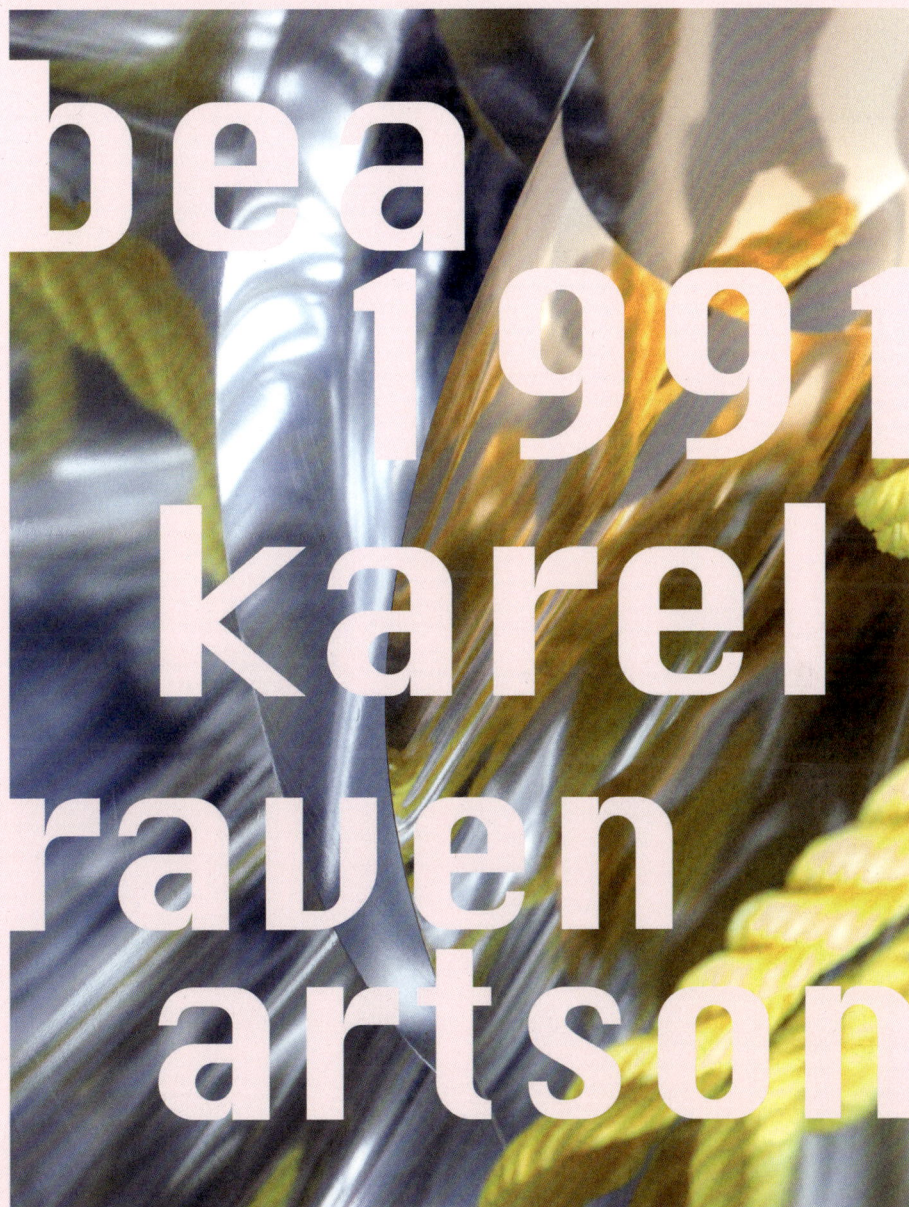

bea
1991
karel
raven
artson

20.07

21:00
internet explorer

Windows 98 (DJ)
Gurr (DJ)
Butterfly Hour (DJ)
S/L (DJ)

Shameless/Limitless proudly presents
a happening as unlikely as it is exceptional
with DJs

Windows 98 (Win Butler of Arcade Fire)
Gurr
Butterfly Hour
maybe some surprises too.

Limited capacity — plan accordingly.

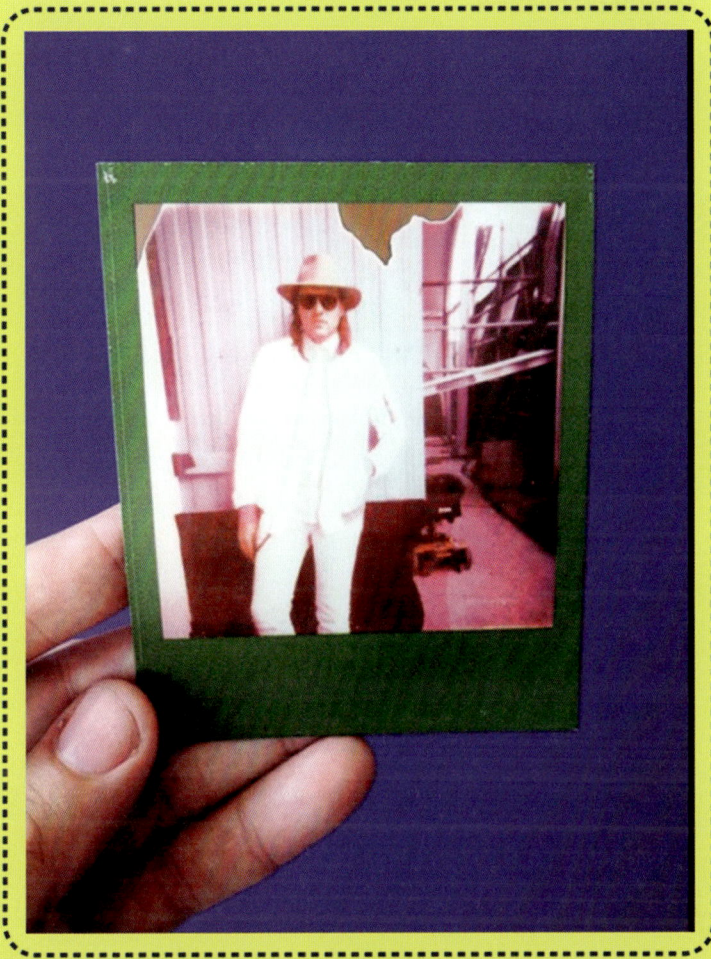

DJ Windows 98
(Win Butler of Arcade Fire)

GURR
(DJ, Berlin)

Butterfly Hour
(Berlin)

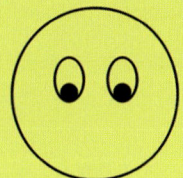

SHAMELESS
/LIMITLESS

14.08.2018
20:30
Ziegrastraße 11 12057

Cadence Weapon
Sean Nicholas Savage
Molly Nilsson (DJ)

This hot show in local area includes live performances from
Cadence Weapon (aka Edmonton's poet laureate)
Sean Nicholas Savage (aka Neukölln's charming prince)
and also
to sweeten the deal
Molly Nilsson (aka no.1 by every conceivable and imaginable metric) is DJing.

It's at Internet Explorer and we'd all be richer if you came. Please come.

shameless/limitless presents...
CADENCE WEAPON
SEANICHOLASAVAGE
LIVE IN BERLIN
with DJ MOLLY NILSSON
AT INTERNET EXPLORER
THURSDAY AUGUST 23 2018
20:30

infinite bisous
Jason Harvey
Fantasy Fiction (DJ)

DAS GIFT
AFTER PARTY

infinite bisous (DJ)

Well now,
here's something to feel good about, at least in the short term:
infinite bisous, the project of the multi-talented
soft soul sole mate songwriter Rory McCarthy
is coming back to Berlin. Full band, hot new material,
buy buy buy.

Beloved by all and beholden to none, innovator and
video maker Jason Harvey is going to do a tight 20—50
minute comedy set to open the night.

Fantasy Fiction Records will DJ before and between.

Shameless/Limitless: infinite bisous After Party & DJ Set
at Das Gift is happening post-show.

Rory McCarthy

16/09/18
shameless/limitless
presents:

infinite bisous (paris)
jason harvey (berlin)
20:00
- marie antoinette
after-party
infinite bisous dj set
das gift

RORY MCCARTHY
Designer
infinite bisous

I have long been committed to the
sweatboxes of Europe.

Loophole, mid-summer in Berlin, 2016,
reached such heights of condensation
that it became something else. As we
played, the sweatbox morphed into
the kind of moist cave that sages
would ardently practice in, like a
scene from Lourdes.

After our show finished, the holy
grotto became a kind of "speaker's
corner" for any man or woman with
wise words to preach, the most
memorable of which was famed
skateboarder Dustin Dollin, who —
from a scribbled piece of paper from
his pocket — rapped, or maybe sang.
I don't remember.

Jack Chosef
Schwund
Mark Stroemich (DJ)
Vero Manchego (DJ)
S/L (DJ)

May all those in attendance at this Shameless/Limitless event fully and
completely enjoy the primal force and life-affirming celebration of song,
community and potential performed live by the capable and captivating

Jack Chosef
Schwund

as well as the selections of Neukölln artists in residence and long-
established professional partiers

Mark Stroemich
Vero Manchego

and also prob some S/L MP3s off the start to set the mood.

Chloë Galea

SHAMELESS / LIMITLESS

presents

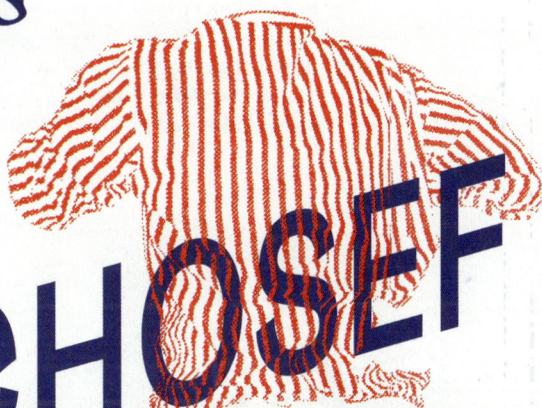

JACK CHOSEF

Berlin

SCHWUND

Berllin

+ DJs

MARK Berlin
STROEMICH
VERO Berlin
MANCHEGO

LOOP HOLE

22.09

2018

23h

Molly Nilsson
Magic Island
Rhi Rhi (DJ)

SAMEHEADS
AFTER PARTY

Magic Island (DJ)
L. Zylberberg (DJ)
Apostille (DJ)

MOLLY NILSSON

2020

RECORD RELEASE SHOW

WITH

MAGIC ISLAND

OCTOBER 21

8PM

HEIMATHAFEN NEUKOELLN

SAMEHEADS

OCTOBER 21 ~ 10:30PM

APOSTILLE

L.ZYLBERBERG

MAGIC ISLAND

DJS

AFTER SHOW PARTY

MOLLY NILSSON

2018 10 26   LOOPHOLE

                  Linda Fox
                  Discovery Zone
                  Farao (DJ)
                  DJ Moyes
                  S/L (DJ)

Tabitha Swanson

☺ 26/10/18 @ 22:00 @ Loophole ☺

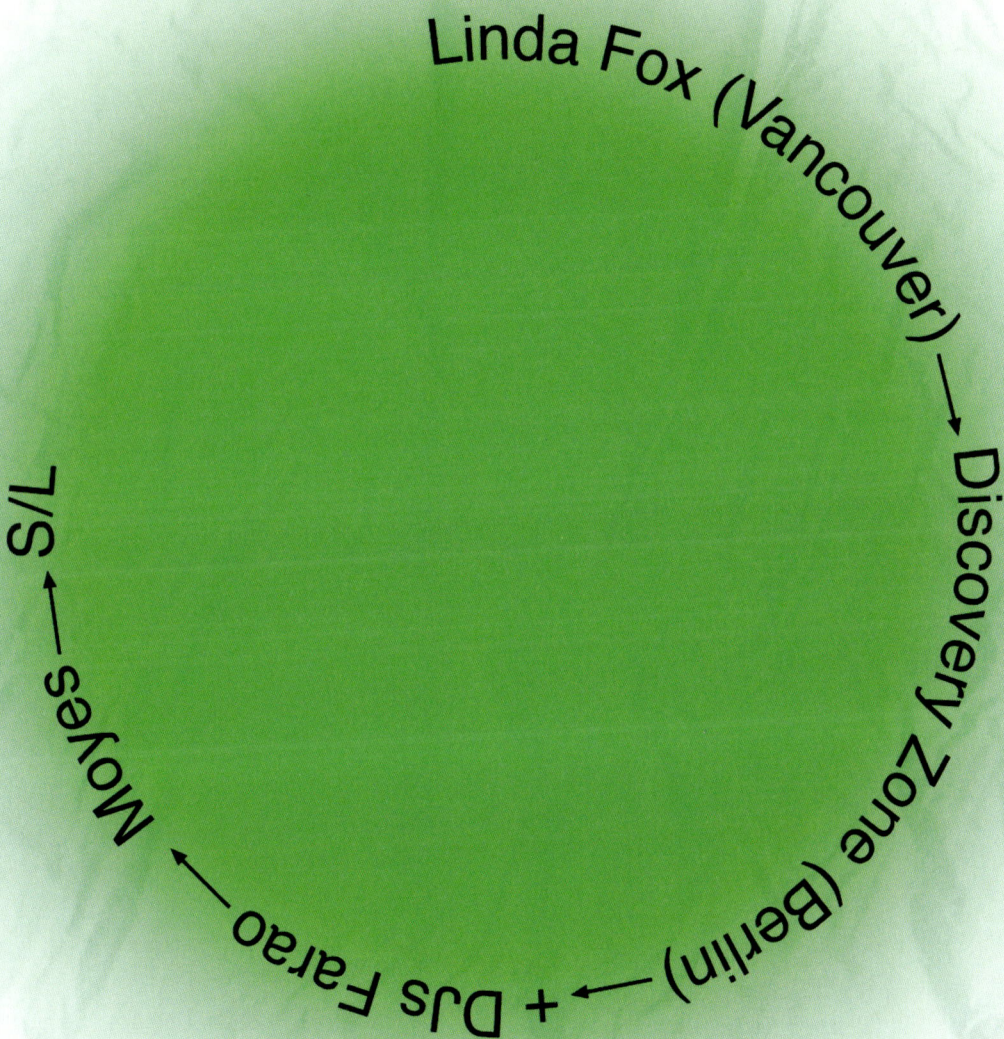

Linda Fox (Vancouver) → Discovery Zone (Berlin) + DJs Farao → Moyes → S/L

Donny Benét
Karolini
DJ bathroom selfie

Shameless/Limitless
presents

DONNY BENÉT
(SYDNEY)

WITH KAROLINI (BERLIN)

04.11.18
20:00
URBAN SPREE

dot dash
RemoteControl
Lullaby factory BOOKING
POWERLINE AGENCY

Better Person
Idiott Smith
Jaakko Eino Kalevi (DJ)

Better Person is working on it:

— He's got a few new songs that he'd like to share.

— He's enlisted a sax player who goes by Jess Gililand to further enhance
the BP live experience. Hi Jess.

— He called across the range to invite his friend Idiott Smith in Groningen
to play support and his friend Idiott Smith in Groningen said yes.

— He said "Hey Jaakko Eino Kalevi, you wanna DJ?"
I wouldn't be telling you about it if the answer weren't yes.

He's getting there. Let's go there together.

Nov 15 at www explorer.

Please come.

Steffen Ullmann

Shameless/Limitless Presents...

BETTER PERSON

IDIOT SMITH
Groningen

Mansions & Millions, Berlin

JAAKKO EINO KALEVI Dj

15/11/18
20:30h
Internet Explorer

© Steffen Ullmann

2018 12 06   LOOPHOLE

               GENTS
               LIA LIA
               S/L (DJ)

My people,
Copenhagen's GENTS are releasing a slow drip of new material
and it seemed like a good idea to everyone in the room
at the time
to celebrate that reality
with a Loophole show.

Prove us right.

Support comes courtesy of LIA LIA, newly returned from
an extended stay in beautiful Los Angeles, California.

Please come.

Christopher Burrows

SHAMELESS LIMITLESS

06.12.18

LOOP HOLE

20:30

GENTS
(Copenhagen)

LIA LIA
(Berlin)

INTERNET EXPLORER
            SCHRIPPE HAWAII
            10 YEARS SHAMELESS/LIMITLESS

            Bad Hammer
            John Moods
            Magic Island
            Sean Nicholas Savage
            Skiing (Cancelled)
            Bea1991 (DJ)
            DJ Moyes
            infinite bisous (DJ)
            LINNÉA (DJ)
            Lolsnake (DJ)
            Molly Nilsson (DJ)

Celebrating 10 Years of Shameless/Limitless.
Celebrating 10 Years of success.

Spread over 2 floors at Ziegrastraße 11

W/

Live:
Bad Hammer
John Moods
Magic Island
Sean Nicholas Savage

DJs
Bea1991
infinite bisous
LINNÉA
Lolsnake
Molly Nilsson
Moyes

Please come again.

Norman Palm

KEVIN HALPIN'S

SHAMELESS
LIMITLESS
10 Years of Success

LIVE
BAD HAMMER
JOHN MOODS
MAGIC ISLAND
SEAN NICHOLAS SAVAGE
SKIING
DJs
BEA1991
INFINITE BISOUS
LINNÉA
LOLSNAKE
MOLLY NILSSON
MOYES

8.12.2018
ZIEGRASTR. 11
22:00

TWO FLOORS!

2019 01 10   LOOPHOLE

          Jackson MacIntosh
          John Moods
          Martha Rose (DJ)

Lou Hillereau

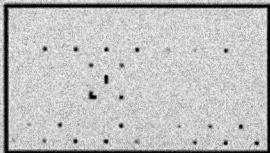

SHAMELESS
LIMITLESS ⚡
PRESENTS

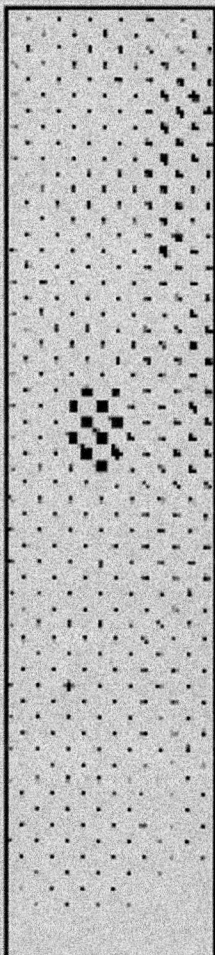

JACKSON MACINTOSH (of TOPS, Los Angeles)
JOHN MOODS (Misantone & Milliona, Berlin) MARTHA ROSE (DJ, Berlin)

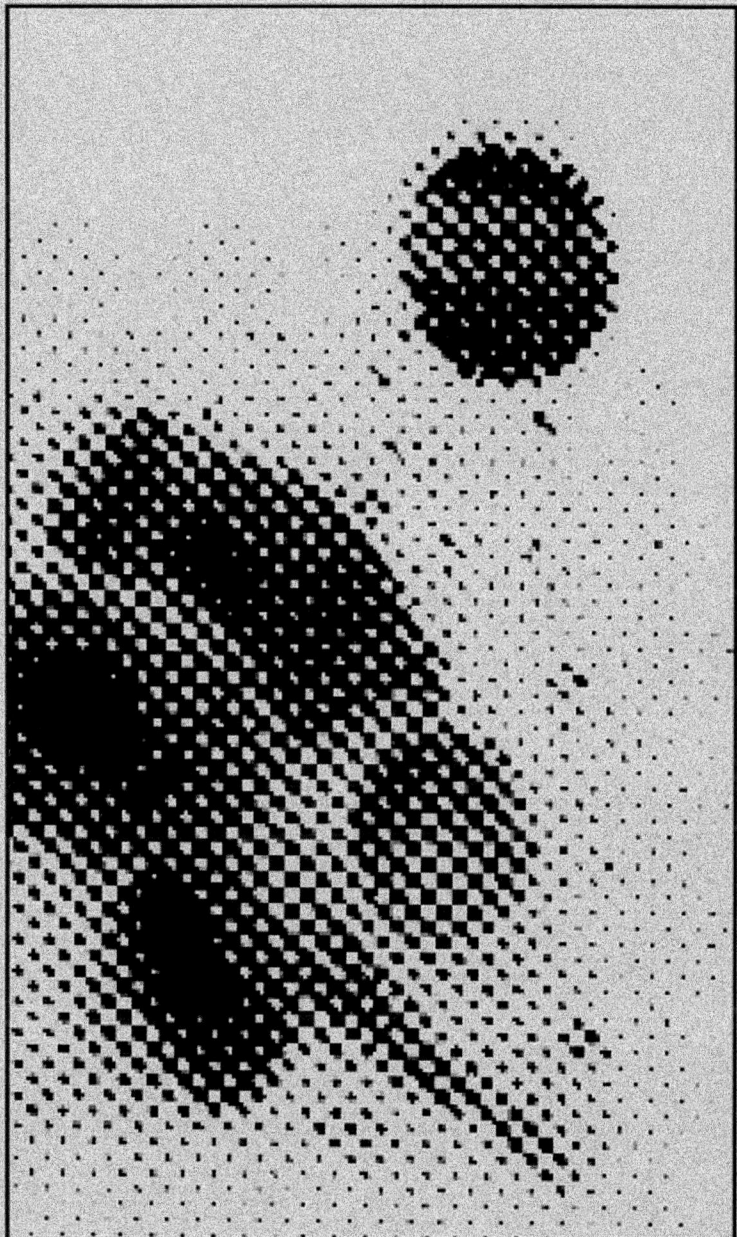

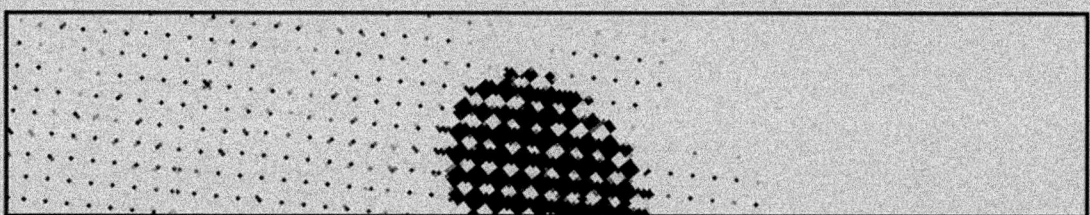

10/01/2019 20:30 LOOPHOLE

Farao
Jae Tyler
Baal & Mortimer

If you're looking for words to generate excitement and enthusiasm ahead of
Farao's Berlin stop on her Pure-O album tour, you're looking in the wrong
spot, my friend. Let me instead direct you to what brought me here, and
what will bring you to Marie-Antoinette this Jan 24: the zither-infused,
disco-tinged perfect pop songs.

They're online, ready for your keen ear and ensuing broad smile. Stream
'em now for a taste, show up to the show for the real — maybe better than
the real — thing.

With support from recent Amplify Berlin enlistee Baal & Mortimer and also
power pop party person Jae Tyler.

Farao

LIVE! LIVE! LIVE! LIVE! LIVE! LIVE! LIVE!
FARAO
SUPPORT: JAE TYLER + BAAL & MORTIMER
MARIE ANTOINETTE
24 JANUARY 2019
DOORS: 20.00
LANDSTREICHER KONZERTE
ASK HEL MUT
@FARAOMUSIC
M/R
SHAMELESS /LIMITLESS

SÖREN BILL
Internet Explorer
Tennis Bar

went to a couple of Shameless/Limitless shows back in the day, at Loophole or WestGermany probably, and to be honest most of what I saw wasn't really my thing: people singing and dancing to backing tracks. For me it was still the time of bands, so this totally affronted my idea of live music. Still, even back then, long before my conversion, I kind of always had a good time at those events. Was it the vibe? The people? The cheap drinks? The radical un-ashamedness of those performances?

When I started Internet Explorer in 2017, I knew I wanted S/L to put on shows there. I bluntly asked, and simple as these things go with the S/L spirit, we started working together pretty quickly, and on a regular basis.

Internet Explorer wouldn't have been anything like what it was without S/L, and many of my all-time concert highlights there were S/L nights: John Moods backed by The Hole Boys, Molly Nilsson, Crack Cloud, and the S/L 10-Year Anniversary.

While a lot of shows and general organization at IE were messy and stressful, S/L events turned out to be a safe bet: smooth communication, a clear outline, reasonable schedules, friendly customers and a sincerely positive attitude – certainly and by far the most professional DIY promoter I had the pleasure to work with!

On top of that, I soon came to understand and eventually love the musical delights S/L represents! Not that it is a certain genre or style nor is it all just backing track performances; it's much more some kind of special quality and a forward-looking momentum underlying it all. It's very important to me to state that besides being a very well functioning operation, to me S/L is at its core a visionary aesthetic platform providing space for creative outlets of true value. In doing so it's shaping the musical landscape of Neukölln, Berlin, and definitely far beyond.

Jason Harvey
Dylan Aiello

Hey guys welcome to the facebook event glad you're here please
feel welcome.

So we're gonna do it a little differently this time. In lieu of the
normal half-baked hype talk in which the fact that in addition to this
being primarily a celebration of the release of Jason Harvey's new
novel at which the author will be reading with piano accompaniment
courtesy of Adam Byczkowski, and it also being a place at which the
#ultrarare Dylan Aiello will speak publicly, I'm gonna pass off the mic
to the man of the hour himself to say some words take it away Jayyce:

hi it's me Jason H
i made a small book here
we will "release" it here
at a new hot local sports bar "Tennis" (basement)
at this party
i will read from book, and create
a small but immersive digital
multimedia experience
Adam Byczkowski will also play piano at the same time very quiet
pls god i hope you think about 'attending'
thank u for reading

:)

hi it's me Jason H
i made a small book here
we will "release" it here
at this party
i will read from book, and create
a small but immersive digital
multimedia experience

feat.Adam "DADDY" Byczkowski (from music)

hello

Please I am begging you to come
or at least think about coming to this event

enigmatic artist Dylan Aiello will also make
a performance

Suggested price

560€

Thoughtful
professional
meditations

the small book looks like this (36 pages)

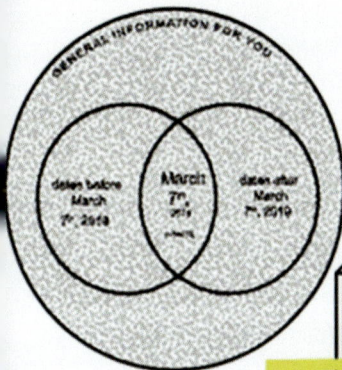

GENERAL INFORMATION FOR YOU

dates before March 7th 2019

March 7th 2019 only

dates after March 7th, 2019

here is a schematic of the bar "Tennis"
i made from memeory

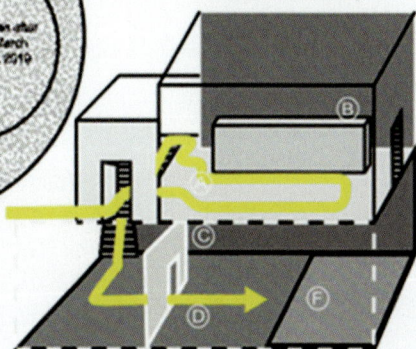

LEGEND

A door to outer area
B commercial zone
C stairs
D liminal area
E humble stage
F proceed to dungeon
G toilet and wasing area

BERLIN!

SHAMELESS
LIMITLESS

tennis

ΙΑΣΟΝΑΣ

das bisschen Totschlag
Aporia
S/L (DJ)

Shameless/Limitless warmly welcomes to the stage the next gen of soft-rock avant-pop post-schlager advocates: Amsterdam's das bisschen Totschlag (Berlin debut!) and Berlin's very own Aporia (new chunes!).

Sam Stevenson

SHAMELESS/LIMITLESS prese

28 March 2019

20:30

Loophole

das bisschen

Totschlag

Aporia

(Amsterdam)

(Berlin)

Otha
Grip Tight
Juno Francis (DJ)

Daria Melnikova

SHAMELESS LIMITLESS

2 apr - 20:30 Loophole

HOT

oslo

GRITIGHT

berlin

Bad Hammer
Two Gospels
Henry 3000 (DJ)

SHAMELESS/LIMITLESS
PRESENTS

BAD HAMMER
EXTENDED PLAY RELEASE SHOW

FEAT.
TWO GOSPELS (LIVE)

HENRY 3000
(DJ/DOOM CHAKRA TAPES)

11. APRIL 2019 WEST GERMANY

Palmbomen II

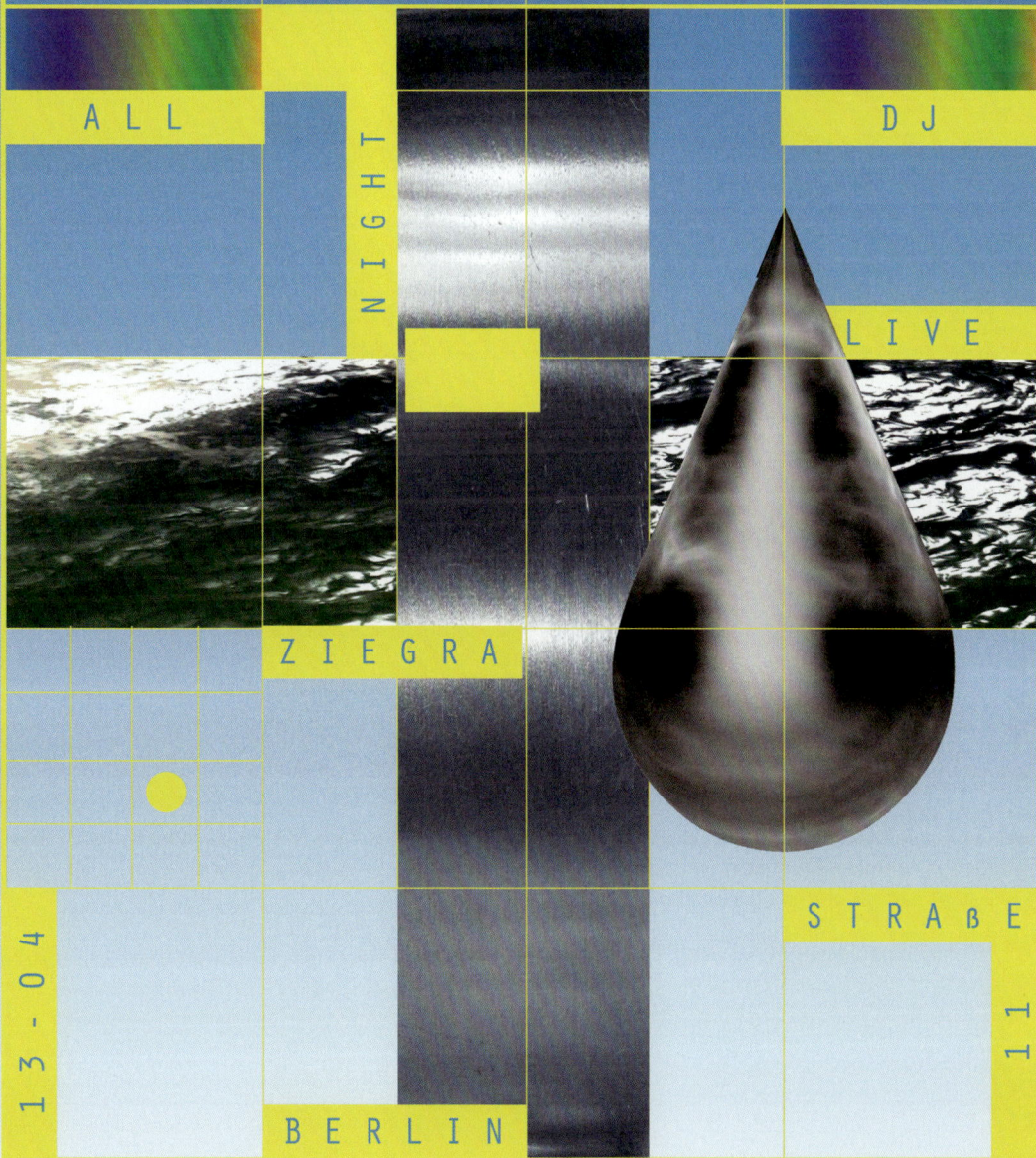

A Tribute To February Montaine
Discovery Zone
Fantasy Fiction Records (DJ)

In celebration of
and appreciation for
February Montaine's
life and times and work and music,
Shameless/Limitless brings you
a séance
and live performance
both of which will be lead by chief Montaine
advocate Sam Potter (ex Late Of The Pier).

The function will triple as the record release for
As Late As The Light That Hides It,
a compilation of Montaine's newly discovered
and remixed home recordings, out Feb 28 via
Fantasy Fiction Records.

Discovery Zone will be present physically and celestially throughout,
and in a performative manner at the evening's outset as well. Fantasy
Fiction will DJ as called upon.

Jason Harvey & Sam Potter

February Montaine

ALBUM RELEASE SHOW AND SEANCE
+ DISCOVERY ZONE (BERLIN)
+ FANTASY FICTION DJS
= TENNIS 17.04.2019 20:30

SHAMELESS /LIMITLESS

© Linda Fox
Juno Francis
Educated Body (DJ)

Ilona Russell

© Linda Fox (Vancouver)
Juno Francis (Berlin)
Educated Body (DJ)
Internet Explorer
20:30
02/05/2019

SHAMELESS ⚡
LIMITLESS ⚡

Jae Tyler
Polje
A'KARI (DJ)

What we've got here
what we're aiming to achieve
what's being executed
dutifully and daringly and glaringly
is a celebration
on the occasion
of power pop party provocateur Jae Tyler
releasing a 12" double A-side
featuring the tracks
"Exercise" & "Nuclear Holocaust Party Anthem 2021"

This can't be achieved
or executed
with duty and daring
in a matter some consider glaring
without you.

Worn Pop affiliate Polje is coming over from Kiev to play support.

A'KARI will DJ before and after the show.

And so: please come.

Sigurlaug Gísladóttir

Erika de Casier
Special-K
Seb (DJ)

Erika de Casier & Natal Zaks

new album by Erika de Casier:

ESSENTIALS

release concert

Performing artists:

Erika de Casier
from copenhagen

SPECIAL-K
from berlin

SEB
dj, berlin

ESSENTIALS

PRESENTED BY

SHAMELESS/LIMITLESS

The 4th of June 2019, 20:30 at Internet Explorer

SEAN NICHOLAS SAVAGE
Artist
Designer

There have been so many incredible Shameless nights over the years, big ones but also really inspiring modest shows too, those are my favourites sometimes. If I just need to get out, and show up alone to see something more intimate, many times I have walked away deeply affected.

In June last year, 2019, my brother visited me in Europe for the first time. I've lived away from home a long time actually, people don't make it over so often, so it was kind of special, and one night we went to a Shameless show. It was Pascale Project and Antoine93 from Montreal, two really amazing and fun acts. We walked from Hermannplatz. I was drinking a big bottle of red wine I think, and we were singing and shouting all the way there.

When we got to Internet Explorer it was a pretty slammin' scene, like lots of friends and funky people out, which is not so unusual I guess. Both acts were super exciting that night. My brother and I danced our hearts out through each set.

He's a few years older than me, and used to go to raves and everything in the '90s when I was too young for that. I just remember at one point, him turning to me and screaming that this was the coolest party he'd ever been to in his life. Haha and I was just laughing my head off, I was pretty tickled about that statement.

I looked around and thought, "Ya, maybe it is."

Pascale Project
Antoine93
Soft as Snow
DJ Moyes
DJ Kowboj

It's this:
Pascale Project
Antoine93
and
Soft as Snow
are going to play live
and
DJs Moyes and Kowboj
are DJs so they're gonna do that
on a Saturday night in June
at community rec room Internet Explorer.

Made possible with the generous support of Shameless/Limitless.

Please come.

Pascale Mercier

SIL - WORLDWIDE - SIL

presents...

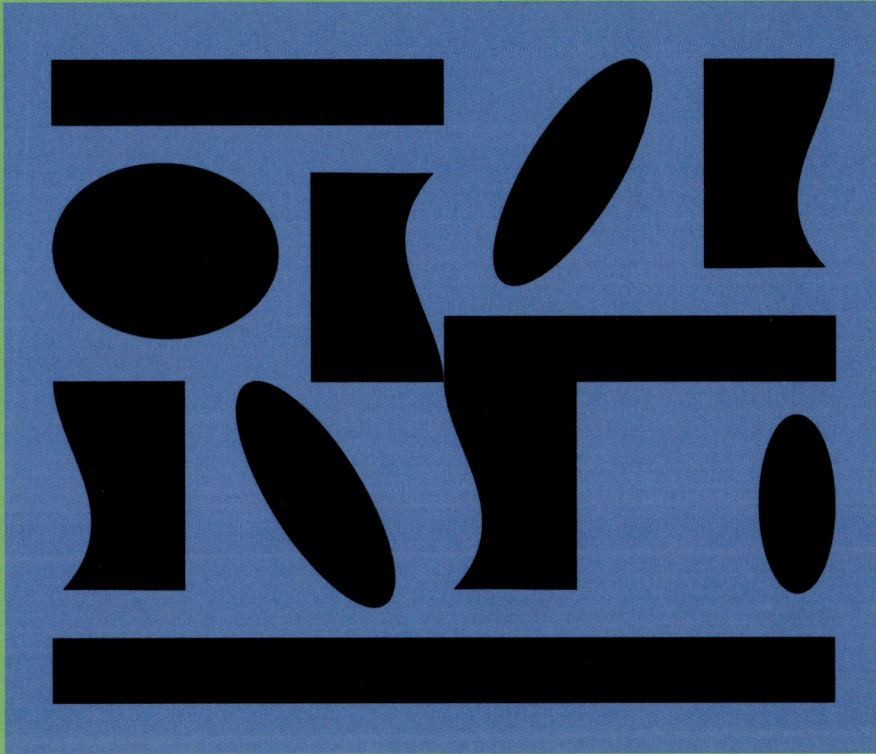

PASCALE PROJECT (MONTREAL)
ANTOINE93 (MONTREAL)
SOFT AS SNOW (HOUNDSTOOTH, BERLIN)
DJ KOWBOJ & DJ MOYES

08/06/19 INTERNET EXPLORER 9PM

Hélène Barbier
Kristian North
New Young Panni Club (DJ)

SHAMELESS ⚡ LIMITLESS

HÉLÈNE BARBIER

(montréal)

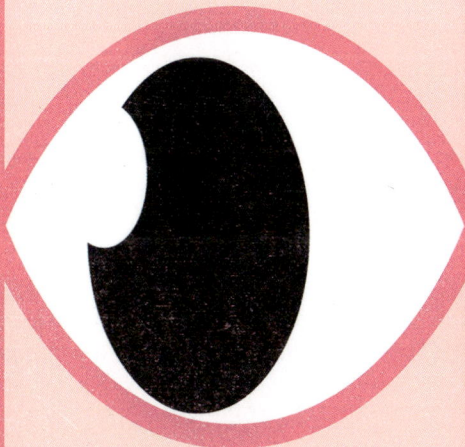

KRISTIAN NORTH

(montréal)

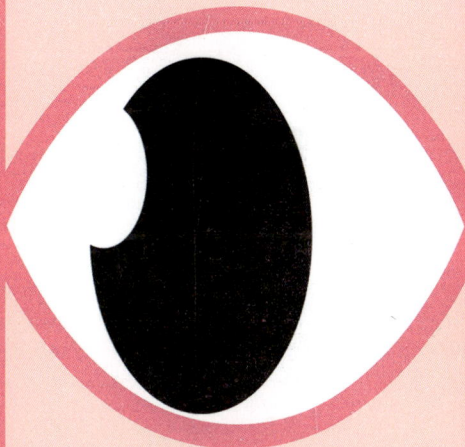

13/06 2019

20:30 LOOPHOLE

Kirin J Callinan
Faux Real

KIRIN J CALLINAN
FR 05.07.2019
BERLIN - URBAN SPREE

facebook.com/KirinJCallinan
meltbooking.com

SHAMELESS
LIMITLESS

MELT!
BOOKING

Donny Benét
Big Mike

Crack Cloud
Amigdala
Military Genius

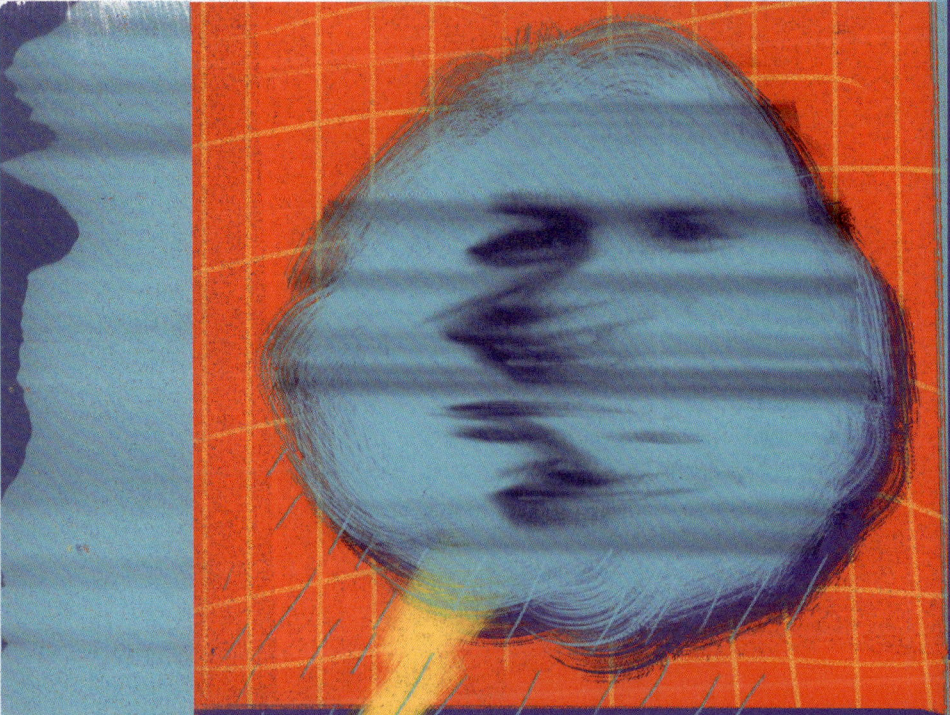

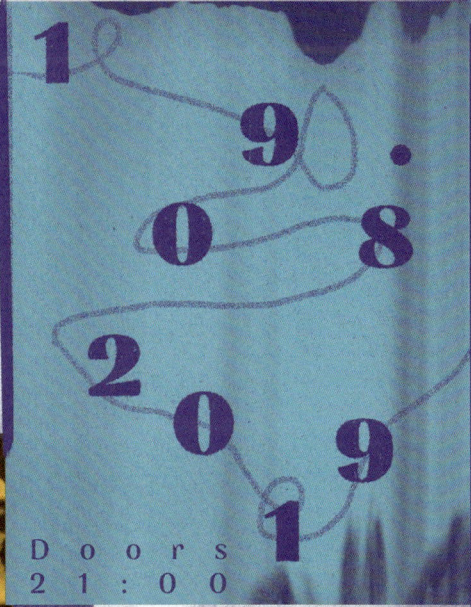

Oscar Key Sung
slimgirl fat
Jasper Lotti
DJ Stiletto

Shameless/Limitless presents:

Oscar Key Sung *(melbourne)*

slimgirl fat *(berlin)*

JASPER LOTTI

(los angeles)

29.08.19
20:30 at Internet Explorer

LIA LIA
Ghost, I
Toasty (DJ)

BOBA BOBA
MUSIC VIDEO RELEASE PARTY

THURSDAY 5TH OF SEPTEMBER
AT FITZROY IN BERLIN, HOLZMARKTSTRASSE 15-18
DOORS: 20:00 UHR
LIVE PERFORMANCES BY LIA LIA & GHOST, I
DJ SET BY TOASTY

FITZ ROY

SHAMELESS LIMITLESS⚡

Alex Cameron
Jack Ladder

LOOPHOLE
AFTER PARTY

Alex Cameron (DJ)
Roy Molloy (DJ)
Jack Ladder (DJ)
Bad Hammer (DJ)

After the fireworks over the sea
and the oyster buffet that will be
Alex Cameron + Jack Ladder @ Festsaal Kreuzberg,
please join the crowd
and head in the direction of Loophole
for the Al Cam tsunami afterparty,
featuring DJs
Alex Cameron
Roy Molloy
Jack Ladder
and
Bad Hammer.

Alex Cameron

UND JACK LADDER AM 16. OKTOBER
LIVE IM FESTSAAL KREUZBERG

Afterparty mit DJs Alex Cameron, Roy Molloy, Jack Ladder & Bad Hammer im Loophole

POWERLINE AGENCY

SHAMELESS LIMITLESS

GREYZONE

Sean Nicholas Savage
Two Gospels
S/L (DJ)

Shameless/Limitless proudly presents
the
iconic
irreverent
indisputably unique
and uniquely talented
Arbutus Records-signed
poet, songwriter and performer extraordinaire,
the one and only
Sean Nicholas Savage
for an Oct 30th engagement
at
Berlin DIY's most elegant venue
Marie-Antoinette.

Support comes courtesy of
Berlin-based up-and-comer
Two Gospels.

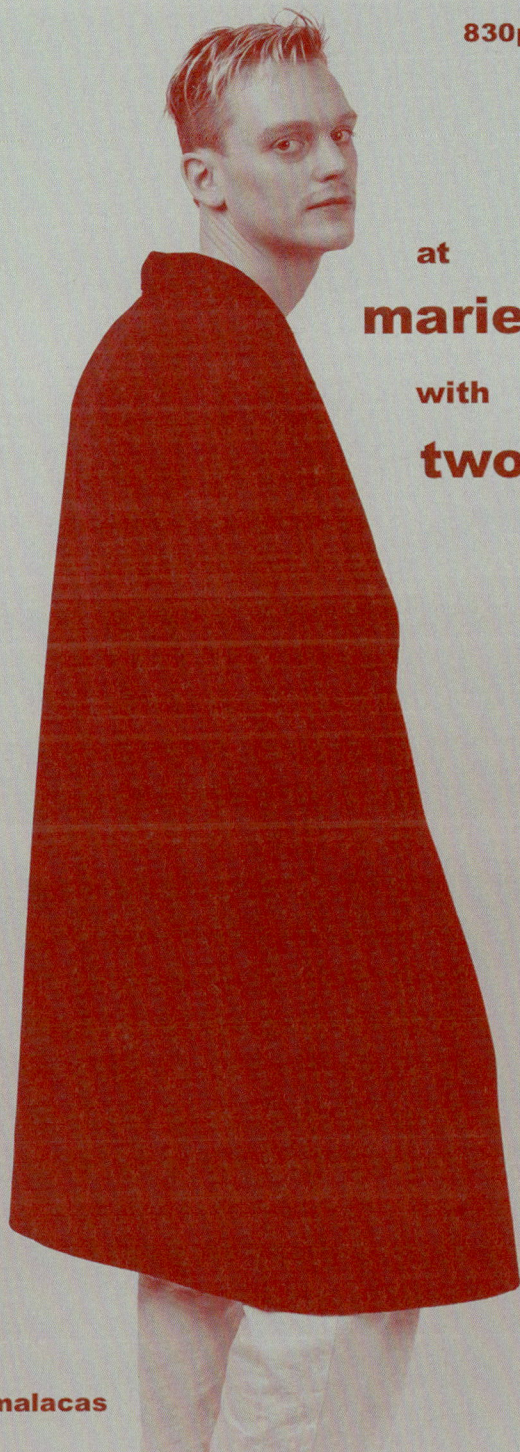

seanicholasavage

performing in berlin october 30 2019

830pm

at

marie antoinette

with

two gospels

shameless
/limitless

photo by pedro malacas

KARI JAHNSEN
Designer
Farao
Street Pulse Records
Ultraflex

It was one of those perfect
nights: Ultraflex were supporting
Jae Tyler for his album release
at WestGermany and of course S/L
had done a kick-ass job of making
sure the room was packed. We got
the room nice and steamy before
Jae Tyler's set – everything went
right and the vibe was spectacular.
There were so many familiar faces
in the crowd but also a bunch of
people I'd never seen before,
which made me realise the word
was out. Little did we know it
would be the last gig we played
or saw before everything went to
shit and the world locked down …
It makes the memory even more
special.

Bad Hammer
Circular Ruins
The Pleasure Majenta
S/L (DJ)

Shameless/Limitless proudly presents an evening with Bad Hammer and
friends at Loophole.

Featuring:

Bad Hammer
who are running as smooth and as slick as can be after a cross-continent
run of shows in support of their debut E.P. Extended Play.
+
Circular Ruins
Back from abroad with sharpened instincts, invaluable insights, and the
same good gear that got him working with Portals Editions in the first
place.
+
the south Pacific dark psych stylings of Berlin via New Zealand rock unit
The Pleasure Majenta.

Take note: early show - over by midnight.

Johannes Badzura

BAD   HAMMER
CIRCULAR   RUINS
PLEASURE MAJENTA
09.11.2019 20:00 LOOPHOLE

Early Labyrinth
R&D
Blaue Form

PILLAGING THE RIPE ORCHARDS OF FAITH - SEVERED HEADS CANT SING
SHAMELESS/LIMITLESS PRESENTA • EL ESTRENO MUNDIAL
NOVEMBER 14, 2019
EARLY
DE
LABYRINTH
with special guests:
R&D and BLAUE FORM
at WEST GERMANY
Skalitzer str. 133, Berlin
Doors 20:00 Musik 21:00
SHAMELESS LIMITLESS PRESENTS ANOTHER SKULL SHATTERER - SKALITZER STR. 133, BERLIN
FIGHT POWER NOT PEOPLE - FIGHT WAR NOT WARS EARLY LABYRINTH
GUNS DONT KILL PEOPLE COPS KILL PEOPLE - LIVING PROOF THE SYSTEM WORKS FOR THEM

GENTS
Ultraflex
Magic Island (DJ)

Luis Ake
Jinka
Bad Hammer (DJ)

Luis Ake

John Moods
Gigolo Tears
Amigdala
Lolsnake (DJ)
happy new tears (DJ)
No Drama (DJ)
S/L (DJ)
DJ Darmok

We had joy
We had fun
We had incalculable browser tabs running
Open to shared joy and self-discovery and community building
And the rad tunes
Can't say enough about the rad tunes
But now
The time has come for the modem
To take respite
To reboot
Friends
Shameless/Limitless
and
The Chop
Are logging off
of Internet Explorer.

Not before one last surf supreme though
And this one is supreme indeed
Featuring music from a broad range of URLs
With live shows from
John Moods (Mansions and Millions)
Gigolo Tears
Amigdala
And DJs
Lolsnake (Weeeirdos)
happy new tears (No Shade)
No Drama
S/L
And maybe Darmok too.

Steffen Ullmann

Gigolo Tears
(live)

John Moods
(Mansions & Millions)
(live)

Lolsnake
(Weeeirdos / DJ)

Amigdala
(live)

No Drama
(DJ)

Shameless/Limitless & The Chop
Log Out
of Internet Explorer

happy new tears
(No Shade / DJ)

Internet Explorer

Recycle Bin

S/L   THE CHOP   Internet Explorer   30/11/19   8:00 PM

Jae Tyler
LIA LIA
Giraffi Dog (DJ)
L. Zylberberg (DJ)
Touchy (DJ)
S/L (DJ)

If you like to party then I say come party
at 11 Years Shameless/Limitless, with:

Live:
Jae Tyler (Street Pulse)
LIA LIA

DJs:
Giraffi Dog (Doom Chakra Tapes)
L. Zylberberg (Sameheads / Präsens Editionen)
Touchy (Berlin again!)

Thanks for sticking around
and
MFG,
S/L.

Aisha Franz

11 Years

LIVE:
JAE TYLER
(STREET PULSE)
LIA LIA
Shameless/Limitless

+ DJs

GIRAFFI DOG
(DOOM CHAKRA TAPES)
L. ZYLBERBERG
(SAMEHEADS / PRÄSENS EDITIONEN)
TOUCHY

06/12/19   21:00 LOOPHOLE

Jae Tyler
Ultraflex
S/L (DJ)

STREET PULSE RECORDS & SHAMELESS/LIMITLESS PRESENT...

JAE TYLER DIGEST

ISSUE #1   31 JANUARY 2020

ALBUM RELEASE
FRI, JAN 31
@ WESTGERMANY
DOORS ~20:30

Skalitzer Str. 133/Berlin/Germa...

The Brand New Record!

"My Fans Are 4eva!"

Look at Jae! Do You Like What You See? A Full On Picture Of His Ass – Turn To Page 3!

WITH SUPPORT FROM NEW TEEN SENSATION
ULTRAFLEX©

LOOK!

The New Jae Tyler: He Has Changed!

The first 20 people through the door get a FREE "Fashion Luminescent Electronic Led Colorful Light In The Dark Clock Birthday Gift for Kids Boys and Girls School" wrist watch!!!

"WOW"   "OK"

PARENTAL ADVISORY EXPLICIT CONTENT

<<<click here>>>
@jaetylermusic

Bad Hammer
Pettycash (DJ)

As we enter into 2020, aka the year of the Bad Hammer (and S/L for that matter), it only stands to reason that the band break new ground with new songs at a hometown show in the north's much celebrated 8MM Bar.

And so we're doing just that.

Pettycash (Fantasy Fiction Records) on MP3s post-show.
Maybe before too — come find out.

Johannes Badzura

shameless/limitless
presents

BAD
HAMMER

20.2.2020
20:20
8MMBar

Military Genius
Emma Grace
S/L (DJ)

Military Genius — the solo ambient noise project of Bryce C, who also
does time in Crack Cloud, Nov3l and Blanka — is releasing an LP on Tin
Angel Records on March 6.

Fortuitous timing, that, as it's also the night that MG makes their
return to a Berlin stage, playing the basement of the enduringly loved
Tennis Bar.

Support comes via the contemporary classical Venice-based
composer Emma Grace.

SHAMELESS/LIMITLESS PRESENTS

MILITARY GENIUS *of Crack Cloud and NOV3L*
EMMA GRACE (Venice)   **TENNIS BAR**
06.03.20   20:30H

ALEX CAMERON
Artist

You mighta heard that when you're starting out in show business you need connections. And while that isn't necessarily false, it's the kind of connections that people often get wrong. They think about sending demos to labels, or directly messaging their favourite band hoping they'll get an invite to the circle jerk out behind the tuck shop. Not gonna happen pal. You gotta work if you wanna jerk.

Think of it like this: the industry is full of nine-to-fivers, whether it's labels, agencies or promotion companies – most of them are about as interested in music as the people working at the tax office are interested in tax. They wanna fuck off to the pub or the movies or just bloody home. That's why when people talk about connections they're not talking about a transfer of power, they're talking about a legitimate emotional exchange – business or not, we're dealing in human emotion, storytelling, truths laid bare and examined under hot super trouper-guided lights. They're talking about someone who gets it. Whether they know it or not, they're talking about a friend.

I've worked with a lotta people in my time. Managers who've conned me into publishing deals only to take all the money and disappear down Cambodian dirt bike trails. Agents who take their cut and stash the peanut M&M's in their satchel backstage. I need those M&M's. Some of them make me money. Some of them are good people, with families and genuine love for objectively good music. But none that I'd bike ride around Berlin with at 7 in the morning high on ecstasy looking for a set of house keys. None who I'd introduce to my parents and insist they stay in my childhood bedroom when next adventuring through Australasia. None that I'd trust with my most important asset – my songs and my shows – like I trust the good people at Shameless/Limitless.

No shit, we've gone from 5 people in a gay bar one summer afternoon, to main stage at Berghain with Molly Nilsson, to ramming rooms and nightclubs that steam and sweat with the heaving pulse of a thousand heartbeats. You don't get many good ones like Kevin and his crew. These kinds are lifers. And I stay looking forward to counting out another wet wad of foreign cash at 3AM in the basement of Loophole, rolling up a 5 euro note, looking deep into his eyes, and saying "Hot dog, you did it again."

Rangleklods
Juno Francis

Postponed — new date soon, inshallah

Copenhagen's Rangleklods — formerly the pride of Neukölln, and a key
figure who played a starring role and provided a focused spark of
excellence in Shameless/Limitless's earliest, sloppiest and rowdiest
days — is back to reclaim his crown.

Classics and fresh bakes promised, for the old heads and the dewy-eyed
newbs, let's giver' good for this one.

Support comes via contemporary torchbearers of the Scandinavian touch,
Juno Francis.

Zille Sophie Bostinius

SHAMELESS
LIMITLESS ⚡

PRESENTS
THE RETURN OF

complexions

(COPENHAGEN)

+JUNO FRANCIS
(BERLIN)

Johnny Labelle
Henrich Ferdinand Jelínek

Postponed — new date soon, inshallah

After collaborating with Berlin royalty (Magic Island), opening doors and
windows to Berlin adventurers (Discovery Zone) and building a reputation
with like-minded promoters across the continent (CmptrMthmtcs and beyond),
it is about flippin' time that crown Athenian jewel Johnny Labelle make
his way to Berlin for a Shameless/Limitless show at Loophole.

And that's what this is. This is a facebook event for Johnny Labelle, live
in concert, on Wednesday, April 15, at Loophole Berlin.

Support comes from an ultrarare concert performance from the prince of
Prenzlauer Berg, the eagle of Adlershof, the apple of your eye: Henrich
Ferdinand Jelínek.

Please come.

Léonie Dishaw

20H30
15/04/20

SIL - WORLDWIDE - SIL

//JOHNNY LABELLE
(Athens)
HENRICH FERDINAND
JELINEK (Berlin)///

LOOPHOLE

© LINDA FOX
2019 05 02

18+
2013 04 22

A TRIBE CALLED RED
2013 05 08

**A TRIBUTE TO
FEBRUARY MONTAINE**
2017 10 28
2019 04 17

A'KARI
2019 05 16

ABSOLULU
2014 04 05

AEMONG
2016 10 16
2017 11 04

ALDOUS RH
2016 10 31

ALEX CALDER
2015 11 30

ALEX CAMERON
2014 05 22
2014 06 17
2014 10 28
2015 09 15
2015 10 06
2016 07 28
2016 11 05
2016 11 10
2017 05 26
2017 11 20
2017 12 09
2019 10 16

ALIENATA
2013 05 31

AMIGDALA
2019 08 19
2019 11 30

ANASTASIA FILIPOVNA
2016 05 13

ANDY BOAY
2015 09 18

ANDY WHITE
2014 11 21

ANTOINE93
2015 04 09
2015 07 26
2015 12 11
2017 11 11
2019 06 08

ANTON TEICHMANN
2014 10 15

APORIA
2016 06 29
2019 03 28

APOSTILLE
2015 04 04
2015 09 15
2018 10 21

ARA KOUFAX
2016 08 13

AUTRE NE VEUT
2013 04 22

BAAL & MORTIMER
2017 10 26
2019 01 24

BABE RAINBOW
2011 12 03

BAD HAMMER
2017 08 11
2017 10 26
2018 12 08
2019 04 11
2019 10 16
2019 11 09
2019 11 28
2020 02 20

BAD ORPHAN
2014 07 29

BAHAMIAN MOOR
2015 09 05
2016 03 11

BALCONY DC
2019 09 27–28

BARRY BURNS
2015 09 18

BASKETBALL
2009 06 30
2011 05 01
2011 05 09
2012 04 09

BEA1991
2017 10 01
2018 07 20
2018 12 08

BEAVER SHEPPARD
2013 11 06

BELIEFS
2013 09 26

BEN JACKSON
2015 04 09

BETTER PERSON
2014 06 13
2014 08 30
2015 02 05
2015 04 04
2015 05 28
2016 02 25
2016 10 20
2017 08 11
2017 09 15
2018 11 15

**BETTER PERSON'S
BETTER PERSON**
2015 04 04

BIFIBOY
2015 08 29

BIG MIKE
2019 07 15

BILL KOULIGAS
2014 09 27

BLACKBIRD BLACKBIRD
2011 07 22
2012 05 21

BLANKA
2017 03 22

BLAUE FORM
2019 11 14

BLOOD DIAMONDS
2012 11 14

BLUE HAWAII
2013 09 14
2013 10 04
2016 06 17
2017 11 25

**BLUNTMAN DEEJAY AKA
HOUSE OF DOORS**
2016 03 11

BOBBYPIN
2016 05 28

BODY TOOLS
2015 10 13

BOKONON
2011 01 14
2011 05 01
2011 07 22
2011 12 03

BOMT
2011 09 16

BORN GOLD
2012 05 16

BRIANA MARELA
2017 11 20

BROSHUDA
2016 04 01
2016 08 16

BROTHERTIGER
2012 04 27

BUTTERCLOCK
2011 12 03
2012 02 01

BUTTERFLY HOUR
2017 09 15
2017 10 21
2017 11 08
2018 08 14

CADENCE WEAPON
2018 08 23

CALVIN LOVE
2017 07 21

CAPE
2013 10 10

CAROLINE CLIFFORD
2013 09 26

CFCF
2016 06 17

CHIKISS
2015 06 04

CINDY LEE
2017 04 29

CIRCULAR RUINS
2019 11 09

CITY DRAGON
2013 05 25

CLASSIC MUSCLE
2014 04 05

CLAY HOOVES
2012 07 20
2012 11 14
2013 05 31

**CLOUD BECOMES
YOUR HAND**
2017 04 14

CMON
2018 05 20

CO LA
2013 05 06

COLD CAVE
2013 08 04

**CONQUERING ANIMAL
SOUND**
2013 05 06

COUNTRY
2015 04 09

COVCO
2016 05 13

CRACK CLOUD
2019 08 19

CRIESE
2014 05 10
2015 04 02

CULT DAYS
2017 09 14

CUTICLE
2014 05 10

DALE PHURROUGH
2011 09 16

DALLAS XANAX
2016 10 31

DAN BODAN
2012 11 03
2014 07 11
2015 10 09

DAN YAL
2018 03 17

**DAS BISSCHEN
TOTSCHLAG**
2019 03 28

DAVE I.D.
2014 05 10

DAVID ADDISON
2011 07 22

DEADLIFT
2017 11 25

DENA
2011 09 16
2011 10 21
2014 04 25
2015 11 06

DENT MAY
2013 11 10

DETLEV D. SAASTER
2011 07 22

DEVON WELSH
2016 08 16

DIRTY BEACHES
2012 09 26

DISCOVERY ZONE
2018 10 26
2019 04 17

DIVINE DIAMOND
2015 09 03

DJ ANIMACIÒN

2018 05 11

DJ BATHROOM SELFIE

2018 11 04

DJ BROT

2013 05 08
2013 05 31
2013 09 14

DJ DARMOK

2019 11 30

DJ DEEPMOODS

2015 02 05

DJ JOSHY

2017 10 28

DJ KOWBOJ

2019 06 08

DJ MOYES

2018 10 26
2018 12 08
2019 06 08

DJ RICHARD

2015 05 31

DJ SCHEISSE

2018 05 20

DJ STILETTO

2019 08 29

DOLDRUMS

2012 11 14

DONNY BENÉT

2018 07 09
2018 11 04
2019 07 15

DOOMSQUAD

2013 11 28
2014 05 22
2015 06 02
2016 11 05

DORIS

2018 07 09

DREEA

2013 10 25

DUBAIS

2014 05 15
2014 11 13
2015 04 24
2017 05 23

DYLAN AIELLO

2019 03 07

DYLAN III

2013 06 19
2013 12 13
2014 06 17
2015 12 11

DYSNEA BOYS

2014 11 15

EACH OTHER

2012 11 25

EARLY LABYRINTH

2019 11 14

EAST OF MY YOUTH

2016 11 05

EASTON WEST

2011 09 16

EDUCATED BODY

2016 06 29
2018 03 03
2019 05 02

EMMA GRACE

2020 03 06

ERIKA DE CASIER

2019 06 04

EVY JANE

2014 08 30

EXIT SOMEONE

2016 04 07

FACIT

2014 11 13

FAKA

2017 11 05

FAKE LAUGH

2016 02 14

**FANTASY FICTION
RECORDS**
2018 09 16
2019 04 17

FARAO
2017 11 16
2018 10 26
2019 01 24

FATHER MURPHY
2015 05 05

FATIMA AL QADIRI
2012 07 20

FAUX REAL
2019 07 05

FEELINGS
2014 11 30

FEMMINIELLI NOIR
2013 12 13

FENSTER
2016 05 14
2016 10 14
2017 04 14
2017 11 02
2017 11 11

FOXTROTT
2015 07 26

FRANK FRESHNESS
2013 04 20

FRIENDBOY
2013 12 13

GARY WAR
2013 11 09

GAUNTLET HAIR
2012 02 25

GAVIN RUSSOM
2014 09 27

GENEVA JACUZZI
2016 05 28
2017 10 28

GENTS
2018 12 06
2019 11 26

GHOST, I
2019 09 05

GIGOLO TEARS
2019 11 30

GIRAFFAGE
2013 05 31

GIRAFFI DOG
2019 12 06

GOLDEN DONNA
2014 11 28

GOLDWEINER
2015 04 24

GRAND PRIX
2018 02 21

GREEN FLASH
2012 02 01

GRIP TIGHT
2018 03 20
2019 04 02

GROUP RHODA
2014 05 15

GURR
2018 08 14

HALF GIRL / HALF SICK
2013 05 08

HANDJERKS
2017 11 05

HANDSOME FURS
2011 05 09
2011 09 24
2012 04 09

HAPPY MEALS
2015 04 04

HAPPY NEW TEARS
2019 11 30

HEATSICK
2014 09 27
2016 04 01

HEIMER
2017 09 14

HELEN FRY
2015 06 02
2015 08 29
2017 05 26
2017 09 15
2017 10 05

HÉLÈNE BARBIER
2019 06 13

**HENRICH FERDINAND
JELÍNEK**
2018 02 21
2020 04 15

HENRY 3000
2019 04 11

HOLIDAY SIDEWINDER
2018 03 20

HOMESHAKE
2016 05 14

HONEY HARPER
2017 11 07

HORSE LORDS
2017 04 14

HUSH HUSH
2011 09 16
2012 05 17
2014 10 28

HYAENAS
2013 05 25

IDIOTT SMITH
2018 11 15

INFINITE BISOUS
2016 07 28
2017 01 31
2018 09 16
2018 12 08

ISLAJA
2015 08 27

JAAKKO EINO KALEVI
2013 12 13
2015 06 04
2016 02 23
2016 09 22
2017 05 23

2017 12 09
2018 11 15

JACK CHOSEF
2014 06 13
2015 02 05
2018 09 22

JACK LADDER
2017 05 15
2019 10 16

JACKSON MACINTOSH
2019 01 10

JAE TYLER
2017 11 16
2019 01 24
2019 05 16
2019 12 06
2020 01 31

JAHILIYYA FIELDS
2014 09 26

JAILHOUSE FUCK
2009 06 30

JAMES BOOTH
2018 03 17

JAPANDROIDS
2012 08 29

JASON HARVEY
2014 11 21
2015 09 13
2015 09 18
2015 11 25
2016 07 28
2017 11 11
2018 09 16
2019 03 07

JASPER LOTTI
2019 08 29

JAYYCE
2014 06 13
2014 11 28

JFDR
2016 11 05

JINKA
2018 03 24
2019 11 28

JOE MCMURRAY
2014 11 21
2015 09 18

JOEL ALAS
2014 03 27

JOEY HANSOM
2012 07 20

JOHN MOODS
2018 05 11
2018 12 08
2019 01 10
2019 11 30

JOHNNY LABELLE
2020 04 15

JR SEATON
2013 05 31

JUAN WAUTERS
2014 11 21
2015 09 13

JULIE CHANCE
2013 06 19

JUNO FRANCIS
2019 04 02
2019 05 02
2020 04 02

JUSTIN FREDERICK
2012 08 29

KANDIS WILLIAMS
2013 10 25

KAREL
2018 07 20

KARL MONICA
2015 02 05
2015 11 06

KAROLINI
2015 08 29
2015 09 18
2016 04 07
2017 01 31
2017 05 26
2017 08 11
2017 09 15
2017 11 08
2018 11 04

KELORA
2018 02 17

KEN CHIC
2017 11 08
2018 02 17

KING KHAN
2015 09 13

KIRIN J CALLINAN
2015 11 06
2017 10 01
2019 07 05

KLEIN
2016 05 13

KOOL A.D.
2017 09 14

KOOL THING
2011 07 22
2011 09 24

KRISTIAN NORTH
2019 06 13

KUHRYE-OO
2012 05 16

L. ZYLBERBERG
2018 10 21
2019 12 06

LA CHRONICA
2011 09 24

LAMIN FOFANA
2016 05 13

LAWRENCE ARABIA
2016 09 22

**LE VILLEJUIF
UNDERGROUND**
2018 04 16

LIA LIA
2017 06 29
2018 12 06
2019 09 05
2019 12 06

LIEF HALL
2015 02 05
2015 05 05

LINARDS KULLESS
2011 07 22

LINDA FOX
2018 05 08
2018 10 26

LINDA LEE
2017 07 02
2017 12 09

LINNÉA
2017 11 25
2018 12 08

LINNEA PALMESTÅL
2015 12 11

LOLSNAKE
2018 12 08
2019 11 30

LONG-SAM
2015 06 04

LUI VOETTON
2016 02 14

LUIS AKE
2019 11 28

LUKA
2016 10 31

LUNA LIBRARY
2014 04 06

LX SWEAT
2014 05 10

M.E.S.H.
2014 08 30

MAC DEMARCO
2012 11 25
2014 11 21
2015 09 18
2017 11 08

MAGIC ISLAND
2014 04 08
2014 06 13
2015 02 05
2015 11 21
2016 11 05
2017 06 29

2018 02 21
2018 10 21
2018 12 08
2019 11 26

MAJICAL CLOUDZ
2015 11 25

MAN DUO
2016 10 16
2017 10 05

MANMACHINE
2013 08 14

MANSIONS AND MILLIONS
2016 09 26
2017 03 22

MARCIN MASECKI
2018 03 07

MARI ME
2010 07 30
2011 01 14
2011 02 12
2011 05 01
2011 07 22
2011 09 16
2012 04 27

MARK STROEMICH
2018 09 22

MARKER STARLING
2017 11 02

MARTHA ROSE
2016 09 22
2019 01 10

MATHEMATIQUE
2014 06 13

MATT DIDEMUS
2013 12 13

MATTRESS
2013 06 05

MAX MCFERREN
2015 10 09

MAYA POSTEPSKI
2018 03 17

MELTING HEARTS
2015 08 27
2016 02 23

MÉNAGE À TROIS
2016 10 07
2017 10 21

METRONOMY
2014 04 06

MICHAEL ANISER
2013 05 31

MILITARY GENIUS
2019 08 19
2020 03 06

MINO
2011 09 16
2011 12 03

MISERABLE LESBIANS
2016 05 16

MISTER LIES
2013 05 31

MO PROBS
2014 09 27

MOLLY NILSSON
2012 05 21
2013 06 19
2013 08 14
2013 11 06
2013 12 13
2014 04 25
2014 11 13
2015 04 04
2015 06 04
2015 09 15
2015 09 18
2016 10 07
2016 12 03
2017 05 23
2017 07 02
2017 07 24
2017 09 15
2017 10 21
2018 08 23
2018 10 21
2018 12 08

MONA LISA DISCO
2015 11 21

MOON WHEEL
2013 05 25
2013 12 13
2015 10 13

MOONFACE
2012 05 23

MOSS LIME
2015 11 19

MX WORLD
2016 11 05

N1L
2014 11 28

NAOMI PUNK
2015 01 27

NEMOI
2009 02 21

NEW YOUNG PANNI CLUB
2019 06 13

NICHOLAS KRGOVICH
2017 11 02

NIGHT ANGLES
2014 04 06

NIGHT MUSIK
2015 10 13

NITE JEWEL
2016 09 26

NO DRAMA
2015 09 18
2015 11 06
2016 08 13
2018 03 24
2019 11 30

NO FEAR OF POP
2012 05 16

NO JOY
2013 11 28

NOVELLA
2016 02 14

NÜ SENSAE
2013 04 20

NORMAL ECHO
2014 10 15
2015 02 05

NORMAN PALM
2016 05 28

OOFF-KULTUR DJS
2016 08 13

OFF-KULTUR FESTIVAL
2016 08 31 – 09 02

OGQT
2018 03 24

OH! MEHR!
2010 07 30
2011 02 12
2011 05 01
2011 10 21
2012 05 23
2012 09 26
2013 09 14

OLGA ŻMIEJKO
2016 12 03

OLLE HOLMBERG
2014 11 28

OMEN
2017 04 29

OMER
2015 04 02
2015 09 05
2016 06 17
2016 12 03
2018 03 17

OPERATORS
2016 10 14

OSCAR KEY SUNG
2015 10 06
2017 06 29
2019 08 29

OTHA
2019 04 02

OTIM ALPHA
2018 07 07

PACIFIC STRINGS
2013 06 05

PALE MALE
2013 08 04

PALMBOMEN II
2015 09 05
2016 04 01
2019 04 13

PANNI SIMAI
2018 03 20

PASCALE PROJECT
2017 03 22
2019 06 08

PAULO
2011 09 16

PENDER STREET
STEPPERS
2015 04 02

PETTYCASH
2020 02 20

PHÈDRE
2013 10 10
2014 06 11
2014 07 11
2018 03 24

PHIL FM
2018 02 07

PHILIP FM
2016 02 25

PHYSICAL THERAPY
2015 04 02

PICTORIAL CANDI
2015 11 21
2016 04 07
2016 11 10
2017 07 21
2018 05 11

PIERCE MCGARRY
2014 11 21

PIERS MARTIN
2016 10 16

PISSYPAW
2012 11 03

PLANNINGTOROCK
2015 09 15

PLATTENBAU
2015 01 27
2015 05 26
2016 03 06

POLJE
2019 05 16

PONY
2014 04 08
2014 05 22

PRINCESS CENTURY
2015 11 06

PRIVACY
2014 09 26

PROFESSIONAL YOUTH
2009 02 21

PROJECT PABLO
2015 10 09
2016 03 11
2016 12 03

PROMISE KEEPER
2016 02 25
2016 10 20

PTD
2016 10 14

PURITY RING
2012 11 14

PURPLE PILGRIMS
2013 11 09

PUSCHENREALGOOD
2012 11 25

R&D
2019 11 14

RAFAEL FINNS
2011 12 03

RAISED ON ROBBERY
2016 03 06

RAMZI
2016 06 23

RANGLEKLODS
2011 01 14
2011 05 01
2011 12 03
2020 04 02

RAVEN ARTSON
2018 07 20

REGULAR FANTASY
2016 06 23

REJECTIONS
2013 05 31

RENAISSANCE MAN
2014 09 27

REZZIE AVISSAR
2016 08 13

RHI RHI
2018 10 21

RIP SWIRL
2017 11 25

ROBERT BĘZA
2016 04 07

ROBYN HITCHCOCK
2014 03 27

RODEO
2013 05 31
2014 06 11

ROOMMATEZ
2015 09 18

ROSS ALEXANDER
2018 07 07

ROY MOLLOY
2016 07 28
2017 05 26
2017 12 09
2019 10 16

RROXYMORE
2014 11 13

RUINS OF KRÜGER
2013 04 20

RUSSO
2015 09 03

S/L

2011 05 09
2012 02 25
2012 04 27
2012 05 17
2012 07 20
2012 11 03
2012 11 25
2013 04 22
2013 05 31
2013 06 19
2013 09 14
2013 10 25
2013 12 13
2014 04 06
2014 04 25
2014 11 13
2014 11 15
2015 04 24
2015 09 15
2015 10 29
2016 08 16
2017 01 31
2017 05 15
2017 07 02
2017 09 15
2017 10 01
2017 10 21
2017 11 20
2018 02 17
2018 03 03
2018 03 17
2018 03 24
2018 07 09
2018 08 14
2018 09 22
2018 10 26
2018 12 06
2019 03 28
2019 10 30
2019 11 09
2019 11 30
2019 12 06
2020 01 31
2020 03 06

SABA LOU & OSKA WALD

2018 04 16

SAD EYES

2016 06 29

SAM VANCE-LAW

2018 03 03

SARAH MILES

2016 05 13

SCHWUND

2018 09 22

SCIENTIFIC DREAMZ OF U

2015 10 09
2016 05 13

SEAN NICHOLAS SAVAGE

2013 10 04
2014 04 25
2014 10 15
2015 11 06
2015 11 30
2016 05 12
2016 09 26
2017 07 21
2017 09 15
2018 08 23
2018 12 08
2019 10 30

SEB

2017 05 15
2017 11 07
2019 06 04

SECRET SECRET GIRL

2013 11 28

SEEKAE

2016 04 01

SFTSTPS

2013 05 25
2013 10 10
2014 11 28

SHAMELESS/LIMITLESS

2008
2009 02 12
2009 02 21
2009 06 30
2010 07 30
2011 02 12
2015 06 24 & Every
Second Wednesday
Before & After

SIMON WOJAN

2018 04 16

SISTERS OF SÉANCE

2013 05 25

SKIING

2011 01 14

```
2011 05 01                    TEENGIRL FANTASY
2011 10 21                    2012 02 01
2012 02 25                    2012 07 20
2013 09 26
2014 04 05                    TELEPATHE
2015 04 24                    2013 08 14
2015 11 19
2016 03 06                    TENDRE BICHE
2016 10 07                    2015 11 19
2017 05 23
2017 09 15                    TERROR BIRD
2018 12 08                    2013 06 05

SLIMGIRL FAT AKA              THE BEAT ESCAPE
UGLY DRAGON                   2017 07 24
2018 05 08
2019 08 29                    THE HOLE BOYS
                             2018 05 11
SLOW MAGIC
2013 05 31                    THE PLEASURE MAJENTA
                             2019 11 09
SLOW STEVE
2013 11 10                    THE SETH BOGART SHOW
2015 08 27                    2016 05 16

SMALL BLACK                   THIEVES LIKE US
2013 10 04                    2014 11 21

SODA FABRIC                   TIM KOH
2014 04 05                    2018 05 20

SOFT AS SNOW                  TOASTY
2018 02 17                    2019 09 05
2019 06 08
                             TONSTARTSSBANDHT
SOUNDS OF SISSO               2013 05 08
2018 07 07                    2017 11 04

SPECIAL-K                     TOPS
2019 06 04                    2012 11 03
                             2014 11 30
STROMBOLI                     2015 05 28
2017 04 29                    2017 11 11
                             2017 12 09
SYDNEY VALETTE                2018 07 07
2014 07 29
                             TORN HAWK
TANK                          2014 05 10
2011 09 16                    2014 09 26
                             2015 09 03
TEAMS                         2016 06 17
2014 07 11
                             TOUCHY
TEEN DAZE                     2019 12 06
2012 04 27
2014 04 08                    TOUCHY MOB
                             2012 11 03
```

2013 05 06
2013 10 04
2013 10 25
2013 12 13
2014 07 11
2015 06 02
2015 11 06

TOWN'S SYNDROME
2011 02 12

TWO GOSPELS
2019 04 11
2019 10 30

TY-TAS
2018 07 20

U.S. GIRLS
2015 10 29

ULTRAFLEX
2019 11 26
2020 01 31

UN
2014 07 29

UNHAPPYBIRTHDAY
2013 06 05

VERO MANCHEGO
2013 10 25
2013 12 13
2014 07 11
2018 09 22

VESUVIO SOLO
2016 10 20

VIA APP
2016 04 01

VJ LINARDS
2009 02 21
2011 01 14

VRAIMENT NICE
2017 10 21
2017 12 09

W/NDOWS
2015 09 05
2016 03 11

WALTER TV
2015 09 18

WAND
2015 05 26

WEDDING
2016 05 14

WEEEIRDOS
2017 11 05

WEEKEND MONEY
2017 09 14

WET LOVE$$
2017 10 05
2018 03 07

WEYES BLOOD
2015 11 30

WHITE LUNG
2014 11 15

WHY, ALEX, WHY
2014 08 30
2015 07 26

WINDOWS 98
2017 07 02
2018 08 14

YHA YHA
2018 03 17

YIP DECEIVER
2011 10 21
2012 05 17

YUKI
2011 12 03

ZEN XEN
2018 05 08

AISHA FRANZ
2015 04 02
2015 08 27
2017 11 25
2018 05 11
2019 12 06

ALEXANDER WINKELMANN
2018 11 04
2019 07 15

ALEXANDRA AQUILINA
2016 03 06

AMANDE DAGOD
2014 04 05

ANDRÉAS THORSTENSSON
2013 09 14

ANDY KASSIER
2019 09 05

ANGUS ROSS BAIRD
2016 05 12

ANNA HORVÁTH
2017 03 22

ANTOINE LAHAIE
2015 04 09
2015 12 11

ANTON BENOIS
2013 04 22

ARITA VARŽINSKA
2014 05 15

ATIS JÄKOBSONS
2014 05 15

AXEL KRÜGER
2008

BALY GAUDIN
2016 08 13
2017 11 05

BEN ANDERSON
2016 09 22

BERLIN COMMUNITY RADIO
2016 05 13

BRITTA GOULD
2013 11 28

BRONWYN FORD
2017 08 11

BROSHUDA
2016 04 01
2016 06 17
2016 08 31 – 09 02
2017 07 02
2018 07 07

CARMEN PAULA NEGRELLI
2012 04 09
2012 11 03

CHLOË GALEA
2018 09 22

CHRISTOPHER BURROWS
2018 12 06

CHRISTOPHER KLINE
2019 11 14

CLAIRE POTTER
2008

DAN SHUTT
2016 06 29

DANIELA ROESSLER
2013 06 05

DANIELLE RAHAL
2016 10 16
2018 03 17

DARIA MELNIKOVA
2019 04 02

DAVID ADDISON
2011 09 16
2011 12 03
2012 11 25
2013 10 04
2013 11 10
2014 11 30
2015 06 24

DENITZA TODOROVA
2011 10 21

ELKE FOLTZ
2018 03 07

ENVER HADZIJAJ
2014 09 27

ERIKA DE CASIER
2019 06 04

EVITA VASIĻJEVA
2012 02 01
2013 10 25

FARAO
2019 01 24

FLORIAN BRÄUNLICH
2015 05 05

FRANCES ENYEDY
2014 05 22
2014 07 29
2015 11 19

GENEVIEVE KULESZA
2014 10 28

GRAEME MITCHELL
2008

GUDRUN JONSDOTTIR
2015 04 04
2016 11 05

GUY TORSHER
2014 11 28

HANNE JATHO
2018 07 09

HOLLY MIA
2015 04 24

HUGH FAULKNER
2018 03 20

IAN P. CHRIST
2013 08 04

IEVA KRAULE
2013 05 06

ILONA RUSSELL
2019 05 02

J. LOGAN CORCORAN
2020 01 31

JANA KALGAJEVA
2015 06 04

JASON HARVEY
2014 11 21
2015 09 15
2015 09 18
2015 10 09
2016 12 03
2017 05 23
2017 09 15
2017 11 08
2018 08 14
2019 03 07
2019 04 17

JEONGKYOUNG WOO
2015 08 29

JOAKIM DRESCHER
2012 02 01

JOANNA SZPROCH
2015 06 04

JOE KELLY
2017 10 05

JOEL ALAS
2011 01 14
2013 09 26
2014 03 27

JOHANNA DUMET
2016 10 07

JOHANNES BADZURA
2017 10 26
2019 04 11
2019 11 09
2020 02 20

JORGE H. LOUREIRO
2015 09 03

JÖRN C. OSENBERG
2017 10 01
2017 11 07
2019 07 05

JULIA KIDDER
2018 05 08

JUSTIN WORHAUG
2012 09 26

KAI HUGO
2019 04 13

KARLA PALOMA
2015 11 30

KASPARS GROŠEVS
2016 10 20

KATE MACKESON
2013 08 14
2013 10 10

KELLY DIEPENBROCK
2019 08 29

KEVIN HALPIN
2009 02 12
2009 06 30
2011 05 09
2012 08 29
2015 08 27
2015 10 06
2016 08 16
2017 05 15

L.L
2019 09 05

L. ZYLBERBERG
2013 05 08
2015 05 26

LARS TSCHÖKE
2015 10 29
2016 02 14
2017 09 14

LAUREN LIM
2016 05 28

LÉONIE DISHAW
2020 04 15

LEVI BRUCE
2014 06 13

LEWIS LLOYD
2015 09 13
2016 10 31

LINDA MAI GREEN
2011 02 12
2011 05 01
2012 02 25
2012 11 14
2014 04 25

LIV CARMEN
2016 06 23

LOU HILLEREAU
2019 01 10

LUCAS CHANTRE
2017 04 14
2017 11 02

LUIS AKE
2019 11 28

MAANSI JAIN
2015 10 13

MARIANNA OSTROWSKA
2017 04 29

MARK STROEMICH
2016 03 11

MARTIN DZIALLAS
2017 11 04
2017 11 11
2019 08 19

MATHIAS SCHWARZ
2015 01 27

MAXIMILIAN SCHENKEL
2018 03 03

MIHKEL MARIPUU
2013 11 09

MIKESIAN
2020 03 06

MOLLY NILSSON
2017 07 24

MORITZ FREUDENBERG
2014 04 08
2015 02 05
2015 11 06
2015 11 21
2016 02 25

NATAL ZAKS
2019 06 04

NATALIA PORTNOY
2014 06 11
2014 08 30
2014 09 26
2015 06 02
2016 11 10
2017 05 26

NIALL MICHAEL
JOSEPH GAHAGAN
2017 10 28

NICHOLAS HOUDE
2013 05 25

NORMAN PALM
2015 11 25
2017 11 20
2017 12 09
2018 10 21
2018 12 08
2019 10 16

OLLE HOLMBERG
2014 05 10

OMER SCHWARTZ
2009 02 21
2010 07 30

OSKA WALD
2018 04 16

PASCALE MERCIER
2015 07 26
2019 06 08

PAULA ESTÊVEZ
2014 11 15
2016 10 14

PETER LADD
2008

PICTORIAL CANDI
2016 04 07

RAMI
2013 11 06

RASTAPUNKA
2016 02 23
2016 05 16
2017 10 21

REBECCA MARTIN
2018 07 20

RHIANNE MCNALLY
2014 06 17

RORY MCCARTHY
2016 07 28
2018 09 16

RYAN HAYS
2011 05 01

SAM POTTER
2019 04 17

SAM STEVENSON
2019 03 28

SEANICHOLASAVAGE
2017 07 21
2018 08 23
2019 10 30

SEB HOLL-TRIEU
2016 09 26

SEBASTIAN DÜRER
2018 03 24

SHARMILA BANERJEE
2015 05 28
2017 01 31

SIGURLAUG
GÍSLADÓTTIR
2017 11 16
2019 05 16

SONYA MANDUS
2014 07 11
2014 10 15

STEFFEN ULLMANN
2018 02 21
2018 05 20
2018 11 15
2019 11 30

STEPHANIE HAMER
2019 06 13

TABITHA SWANSON
2017 06 29
2018 02 17
2018 10 26
2019 11 26

THERESA HAGEDORN
2016 05 14

TIM EVE
2015 09 05

TOME ATILLA VIDOŠI
2013 12 13

TONJE THILESEN
2012 05 16

TRENT MANCHUR
2012 04 27

VANESSA KHOURY
2012 05 21

VERONICA MANCHEGO
2011 09 24
2013 06 19
2014 11 13

**VICTORIA
GISBORNE-LAND**
2012 05 17
2013 05 31
2014 04 06

VIKTOR SCHMIDT
2013 04 20

**VIVIANE
CHIL-HAGOPIAN**
2012 05 23
2012 07 20

**ZILLE SOPHIE
BOSTINIUS**
2011 07 22
2020 04 02

8MM BAR
Schönhauser Allee 177B
2020 02 20

ACUD MACHT NEU
Veteranenstraße 21
2014 11 28
2015 11 21
2015 11 25
2016 06 29
2016 11 10
2017 04 29
2017 07 02
2017 09 14
2017 11 05

BERGHAIN
Am Wriezener Bahnhof
2013 06 19
2015 09 15

CAFE WARSCHAU
Sonnenallee 27
2008

CHESTERS
Glogauer Straße 2
2014 07 11
2014 09 27
2014 11 13
2015 02 05
2015 04 02
2015 10 09

CHEZ JACKI
An der Schillingbrücke 3
2011 05 01

DARWIN
S-Bahn Bogen 46
Holzmarktstraße 15
2018 05 08

DAS GIFT
Donaustraße 119
2012 05 23
2012 08 29
2012 09 26
2015 06 24 & Every
Second Wednesday
Before & After
2017 01 31
2018 09 16

DONAU115
Donaustraße 115
2016 08 16
2018 03 07

FESTSAAL KREUZBERG
Am Flutgraben 2
2017 05 23
2019 10 16

FITZROY
S-Bahn Bogen 46
Holzmarktstraße 15
2019 09 05

FREUDENREICH
Sonnenallee 67
2012 11 03

GREENHOUSE
Gottlieb-Dunkel-
Straße 43-44
2015 08 29

HAUS1
Waterloo-Ufer
2011 02 12

HEIMATHAFEN NEUKÖLLN
Karl-Marx-Straße 141
2018 10 21

INTERNET EXPLORER
;)
2017 05 15
2017 06 29
2017 07 24
2017 08 11
2017 10 05
2017 11 02
2017 11 11
2017 11 16
2017 11 25
2017 12 09
2018 03 17
2018 05 11
2018 05 20
2018 07 07
2018 07 20
2018 08 14
2018 08 23
2018 11 15
2018 12 08
2019 04 13
2019 05 02

```
              2019 06 04                          2018 07 09
              2019 06 08                          2018 09 22
              2019 08 19                          2018 10 26
              2019 08 29                          2018 12 06
              2019 11 26                          2019 01 10
              2019 11 30                          2019 03 28
                                                  2019 04 02
        KANTINE AM BERGHAIN                       2019 05 16
      Am Wriezener Bahnhof                        2019 06 13
              2013 10 04                          2019 11 09
              2016 02 23                          2019 11 28
              2017 10 01                          2019 12 06
              2019 07 15                          2020 04 02
                                                  2020 04 15
                    L.U.X
      Schlesische Straße 41                  MARIE-ANTOINETTE
              2009 02 21                 Holzmarktstraße 15-18
                                                  2012 02 25
                    LIDO                          2012 04 09
          Cuvrystraße 7                           2014 04 05
              2017 11 20                          2016 10 16
                                                  2016 10 31
                    LOFT                          2017 04 14
      Bankastræti 7                               2017 07 21
          Reykjavík                               2018 09 16
              2016 11 05                          2019 01 24
                                                  2019 10 30
                LOOPHOLE
      Boddinstraße 60                           MINDPIRATES
              2013 05 25                 Schlesische Straße 38
              2014 06 13                          2011 09 24
              2014 06 17
              2014 07 29                            MONARCH
              2015 04 09                 Skalitzer Straße 134
              2015 04 24                          2012 11 14
              2015 06 02                          2012 11 25
              2015 08 27                          2013 11 10
              2015 09 03                          2014 03 27
              2015 10 06                          2014 05 22
              2015 10 13                          2014 06 11
              2015 11 19                          2014 11 30
              2016 04 07                          2015 09 13
              2016 05 12                          2015 10 29
              2016 06 23                          2016 01 28
              2016 07 28                          2016 03 06
              2016 08 13
              2016 10 20                   MONSTER RONSON'S
              2017 03 11                   ICHIBAN KARAOKE
              2017 03 22                 Warschauer Straße 34
              2017 05 26                          2016 09 22
              2017 09 15
              2017 10 26              NAHERHOLUNG STERNCHEN
              2017 11 07                    Berolinastraße 7
              2018 02 17                          2011 07 22
              2018 02 21                          2011 09 16
              2018 03 20                          2011 10 21
              2018 03 24                          2011 12 03
```

2012 02 01
2012 04 27
2012 05 16
2012 05 21
2012 07 20
2013 04 22
2013 05 31
2013 06 05
2013 08 14
2013 10 10
2014 04 08

NEU WEST BERLIN
Köpenicker Straße 55
2014 10 28

O TANNENBAUM
Sonnenallee 27
2010 07 30

OHM
Köpenicker Straße 70
2014 05 10
2016 05 13

PLATOON KUNSTHALLE
Schönhauser Allee 9
2014 08 30

PRACHTWERK BERLIN
Ganghoferstraße 2
2018 03 03

PRIVATCLUB
Skalitzer Straße 85-86
2015 05 28
2016 05 16

SAMEHEADS
Richardstraße 10
2013 09 14
2013 10 25
2014 04 25
2014 11 21
2015 04 04
2015 09 05
2016 03 11
2016 12 03
2018 10 21

SCHRIPPE HAWAII
;)
2018 12 08

SHIFT
Köpenicker Straße 70
2013 11 06

ST. GEORG
Ritterstraße 26
2016 04 01
2016 06 17

TEAM TITANIC
Flughafenstraße 50
2013 11 09

TENNIS BAR
Reuterstraße 95
2019 03 07
2019 04 17
2020 03 06

URBAN SPREE
Revaler Straße 99
2013 05 06
2013 05 08
2013 08 04
2013 11 28
2013 12 13
2014 04 06
2014 10 15
2015 06 04
2015 07 26
2015 09 18
2015 11 06
2015 12 11
2016 02 25
2016 09 26
2017 05 26
2017 11 08
2018 11 04
2019 07 05

WESTGERMANY
Skalitzer Straße 133
2009 06 30
2011 01 14
2011 05 09
2012 05 17
2013 04 20
2013 09 26
2014 05 15
2014 09 26
2014 11 15
2015 01 27
2015 05 05
2015 05 26
2015 11 30

```
                                    2016 05 14
                                    2016 05 28
                                    2016 10 07
                                    2016 10 14
                                    2017 01 31
                                    2017 10 21
                                    2017 10 28
                                    2017 11 04
                                    2018 04 16
                                    2019 04 11
                                    2019 11 14
                                    2020 01 31
```

YUMA
Reuterstr. 63
2009 02 12

Born and raised in Williams Lake, British Columbia, Kevin Halpin
relocated to Berlin in 2008. Under the name Shameless/Limitless,
and informed by a DIY spirit, he has been independently
organizing concerts, parties, festivals, exhibitions and more
in Berlin and beyond ever since. He lives in Neukölln.

Acolytes, attendees, bartenders, bystanders, colleagues,
contributors, designers, door staff, family, friends, partiers,
players, printers, publishers, sound techs, supporters, well-
wishers, wisdom-givers and the city of Berlin, too: thank you.

IMPRINT

Slanted Publishers UG
(haftungsbeschränkt)
Nebeniusstrasse 10
76137 Karlsruhe
Germany
T +49 (0) 721 85148268
info@slanted.de
slanted.de
@slanted_publishers

ISBN: 978-3-948440-26-8
1st edition 2021

Editor: Kevin Halpin

Consulting: Jana Kalgajeva
Editorial Design: Norman Palm
Printing: Pinguin Druck
Production: Zille Sophie Bostinius
Proofreading: Eric Halpin
Publishing Direction: Lars Harmsen, Julia Kahl

Foreword: Norman Palm talks to Kevin Halpin
Event Texts: Kevin Halpin

Front picture: "10 Years S/L" by Jana Kalgajeva
Credits picture: "Loophole Memory" by Santiago Perez
Back picture: "Glue Recipe #1" by Kevin Halpin

Typefaces: Solenizant, Spot Mono

Thank you to Pinguin Druck GmbH for sponsoring the
publication of this book as part of its "Partner für
Kulturelle Buchprojekte" initiative.

PinguinDruck.de